D1634296

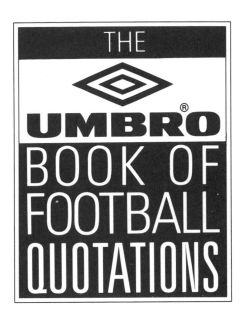

THE

UMBRO®

BOOK OF
FOOTBALL
QUOTATIONS

THE

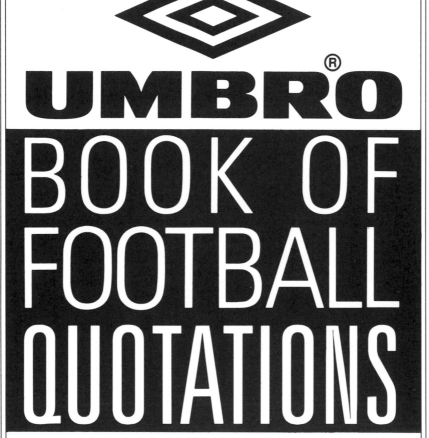

UMBRO®
BOOK OF
FOOTBALL
QUOTATIONS

PETER BALL
A N D
PHIL SHAW

STANLEY PAUL
London

First published 1993

3 5 7 9 10 8 6 4 2

© Peter Ball and Phil Shaw 1993

Peter Ball and Phil Shaw have asserted their right under the Copyright, Designs and
Patents Act 1988 to be identified as the authors of this work

First published in the United Kingdom in 1993 by Stanley Paul Limited
Random House, 20 Vauxhall Bridge Road, London SW1V 2SA

Random House Australia (Pty) Limited
20 Alfred Street, Milsons Point, Sydney,
New South Wales 2061, Australia

Random House New Zealand Limited
18 Poland Road, Glenfield
Auckland 10, New Zealand

Random House South Africa (Pty) Limited
PO Box 337, Bergvlei, South Africa

Random House UK Limited Reg No. 954009

A CIP catalogue record for this book
is available from the British Library

ISBN 0 09 177626 0

Set in Souvenir (Linotron) by Textype Typesetters, Cambridge
Printed and bound in Great Britain by Richard Clay Ltd, Bungay, Suffolk

Contents

Acknowledgements

This book, the fourth edition of the *Book of Football Quotations* and the first with the prestigious support of Umbro, would not have existed but for the efforts of hundreds of others.

Our first thanks are to the players, managers, officials and fans who made it all possible, and especially to those journalists who waited in a rainy street or crowded corridor after a match to record their comments. They are too numerous to name, but every reporter, whether in the national or local media, can take our gratitude as read.

We are particularly indebted for their contributions and interest to a cast of dozens including Mike Alway, Patrick Barclay, Steve Bierley, Roddy Bloomfield, Robert Chalmers, Stuart Cosgrove, Chris Davies, Joe Davies, Jonathan Foster, Daniel Foster, Brian Glanville, Dave Harrison, Graham Hart, Mike Henderson, Bill Johnson, Ken Jones, Hugh Keevins, Simon Kelner, Ken Lawrence, John Lawson, Jim Lawton, John Ley, Joe Lovejoy, Chris Maume, Rupert Metcalf, David Moore, Neil Morton, Eric Musgrave, Kenny MacDonald, Kevin McCarra, Andy McInnes, Alan Nixon, Adrian O'Dolan, Ian Ridley, Ian Ross, Alan Salt, Brian Scott, Martin Smith, Russell Thomas, and Jim Traynor.

Our respective families also deserve thanks for tolerating the project and the intrusive piles of old newspapers it involved, while the enthusiasm of Marion Paull made us delighted to continue a decade-long association with our publishers, Stanley Paul.

Peter Ball, Lancashire
Phil Shaw, Staffordshire
July 1993

Photographic acknowledgement
The authors and publishers would like to thank the following for supplying copyright photgraphs: Colorsport, *The Independent*, All Sport, Bob Thomas Sports Photograghy, Associated Press, Rex Features and Action Images.

CHAPTER 1

The Greats and Others

PLAYERS

Tony Adams

One of the game's great characters.

> GEORGE GRAHAM, Arsenal manager, defending his captain after his imprisonment on a drink-driving charge, *1990*.

I hear Tony Adams is appealing. Apparently he wasn't pissed. He was just trying to get the wall back another 10 yards.

> BOB 'THE CAT' BEVAN, after-dinner speaker, at Football Writers' Association awards night, *1992*.

I thought it was offside – but then I always do.

> ADAMS, on a disputed Southampton goal, *1991*.

Roy Aitken

Big Roy was unbelievable before the game, 'noising up' the Swedes. He told Mo Johnston to spit at Glenn Hysen's feet in the tunnel. Mo said: 'He'll probably trap it and play it up the park.'

> ANDY GORAM, Scotland goalkeeper, recalling his former national captain's motivational powers, *1991*.

John Aldridge

The greatest striker in the world. A perfect pro and a good lad. The sort you'd choose to go to war with.

> JOHN KING, Tranmere manager, *1992*.

Age isn't important except on tombstones and birth certificates. He can still do the business.

> KING, on paying Real Sociedad £250,000 for 35-year-old Aldridge, *1991*.

Dalian Atkinson

I always make sure I write Atkinson D on the teamsheet. Sometimes I wonder if I'm making a mistake.

> RON ATKINSON, Aston Villa manager and 5-a-side player, on his namesake, *1993*.

Franco Baresi

I need more players like Franco, who are on first-name terms with the ball.

AZEGLIO VICINI, Italy coach, on the Milan defender, *1989*.

When people talk about the best players in Europe they tend to go for forwards. For my money, Franco is better than anyone at the moment – including Gullit or anyone else you care to mention.

RAY WILKINS, former Milan team-mate, *1989*.

During the World Cup I accumulated quite a collection of shirts swapped with England's opponents . . . .While all the others stank of sweat, Franco Baresi's No. 2 shirt carried the cool fragrance of Aramis. Italians like to smell nice as well as look good – or is Baresi such a cultured player that he hardly breaks into a sweat?

DAVID PLATT, England midfielder, *1990*.

Nick Barmby

Every scout hopes he spots a genius, but I didn't have to be very clever to pick out Nick.

FRANK CASKEY, **Tottenham scout, *1993*.**

John Barnes

He should be playing for us. He reminds me of a Brazilian player. He can dribble, he has so much skill and he scores goals. He is so special.

CARLOS PERREIRA, Brazil manager, *1992*.

He looks a little fat, slow and lazy.

PELE, *1991*.

The great enigma of international football and the biggest mystery of my career. Why couldn't John Barnes play for England the way he played for Liverpool? I have to admit I don't know . . . . If he was a 'chicken winger' I could have understood it, but we are talking about a brave man, built like a cruiserweight boxer, can't be shifted off the ball, wins headers when the boots are flying.

BOBBY ROBSON, former England manager, in *Against All Odds, 1990*.

And the thought has to be expressed that perhaps the fact that he is Jamaican rather than English comes into it.

JIMMY GREAVES in *The Sun*, World Cup finals, *1990*.

People now talk about him having had eight good games for England out of 58. A few weeks ago it was ten, and maybe soon it'll be down to five. He'll end up thinking he's never had a good game.

GRAHAM TAYLOR, England manager, defending his former Watford protégé, *1990*.

Generally, most things come down the middle, and if you're wide you can be isolated. But positions don't mean that much at Liverpool because when we're playing well, the players rotate. My favourite position, I have decided, is wherever I get the ball.

BARNES in interview with *For Him*, fashion magazine, *1990*.

Earl Barrett

The trouble with Earl is that he's one-paced . . . Zooommm.

JOE ROYLE, Oldham manager, on the centre-half he later sold to Aston Villa, *1990*.

David Batty

Batty would probably get himself booked playing Handel's Largo.

DAVID LACEY, football correspondent, *The Guardian*, after the Leeds midfielder's booking in the Charity Shield, *1992*.

He does not choose to be flash during games, and big names mean nothing to him. When I brought Norman Hunter on to the Leeds coaching staff he was the only one who dared to ask 'Norman who?' That tells you a lot about Batts.

> BILLY BREMNER, former Leeds manager, *1990*.

Jim Baxter

Slim Jim had everything required of a great Scottish footballer. Outrageously skilled, totally irresponsible, supremely arrogant and thick as mince.

> ALASTAIR MACSPORRAN, columnist in Scottish fanzine *The Absolute Game, 1990*.

George Best

The pop cult that grew up around George Best in the Sixties was a far more organic, less contrived process, rooted as it was in a ratio of magnificent performances to adulation that Gascoigne cannot approach . . . . No footballer bred in these islands in my lifetime has come close to rivalling Best's incredible amalgam of gifts.

> HUGH MCILVANNEY, sports writer, *The Observer, 1990*.

The Good, the Bad and the Bubbly

> BEST autobiography title, *1990*.

The best was a blonde girl who arrived and said, 'My car's broken down outside your house. Can I use your phone to call the AA?' I let her in because she was a fair looker. Then I had her on the carpet in the hallway, gave her a quick repair job before the AA man arrived.

> BEST in Michael Parkinson, *George Best, 1970s*.

I've always had a reputation for going missing – Miss England, Miss United Kingdom, Miss World . . . .

> BEST, *1992*.

I spent a lot of my money on booze, birds and fast cars. The rest I just squandered.

> BEST, *1992*.

Noel Blake

A big lad who has muscles in his spit.

> HOWARD WILKINSON, Leeds manager, on the centre-half he sold to Stoke, in *Managing to Succeed: My Life in Football Management,* with David Walker, *1992*.

Pat 'Packie' Bonner

Goalkeepers in Scotland are notorious as 'goal-liners'. If you want them to come off their line you almost have to prise them out with a crowbar. We have asked Packie to be a sweeper.

JACK CHARLTON, Republic of Ireland manager, *1991*.

Scottish goalkeepers are supposed to be bad enough, but an Irish keeper in Scotland . . . . I just had to go out and try and prove everyone wrong.

BONNER recalling early days with Celtic, *1991*.

Liam Brady

The most accomplished player ever to represent the Republic. Giles could set things up for others with a lovely pass, but Brady could do that just as well, and in his younger days could win games off his own back.

EOIN HAND, former Republic of Ireland manager, lamenting Brady's retirement, *1990*.

Billy Bremner

10st of Barbed Wire

SUNDAY TIMES headline on profile of Bremner, *1970*.

Above all [Leeds] have Bremner, the best footballer in the four countries. If every manager in Britain were given his choice of any one player to add to his team some, no doubt, would toy with the idea of Best; but the realists, to a man, would have Bremner.

JOHN ARLOTT, journalist, *The Guardian, 1970*.

Steve Bull

Bull may not have the skill of some, but he's very strong and keeps nudging into you, putting you off balance. We exchanged a few comments during the game but I couldn't understand a word he was saying. That's some accent he's got.

CRAIG SHORT, Notts County defender, *1990*.

If I had a meeting with Bull to discuss every transfer story that appears, I'd have to put a bed in my office.

GRAHAM TURNER, Wolves manager, *1991*.

John Burridge

Hello, this is Scotland's top goalkeeper.

> BURRIDGE, Hibernian's veteran 'keeper, on answerphone message, *1991*.

I've seen him eating jars of baby food before games because he believes it increases his carbohydrate level . . . . He used to describe himself with the words 'I'm as fit as a butcher's dog' – and he is.

> MARK MCGHEE, Reading player-manager, on his ex-Newcastle team-mate's eating habits, *1991*.

Terry Butcher

What character, what stature, what a patriot, what a player!

> BOBBY ROBSON, former England manager, in *Against All Odds, 1990*.

He is passionate about his country. He has stood shoulder to shoulder with every-one since 1982. He has fought for his country all over the world in friendlies, World Cup ties and European Cup matches. He gets involved in a little incident he now regrets and it's blown out of all proportion.

> ROBSON, defending the Rangers defender after he had butted a Tunisian in a World Cup warm-up match, *1990*.

There will be dressing-room doors and walls around Scotland glad to know I've gone.

> BUTCHER, on leaving Scotland to become player-manager of Coventry, *1990*.

John Byrne

He says his hair's natural. He must be using natural bleach.

> PAUL BRACEWELL, Sunderland captain, during FA Cup run, *1992*.

All the stardom has come about five years too late for me and certainly too late for my dad, James. He died just when my career began to take off and missed the best part of it. Maybe he'll be looking down on me at Wembley and send me a goal.

> BYRNE, after scoring in every round up to the FA Cup Final, *1992*. Sunderland's run ended at Wembley.

Eric Cantona

I have the impression that if he cannot score a beautiful goal he'd rather not score.

> MICHEL PLATINI, France manager, *1992*.

We are a team who shout a lot and Eric isn't getting all the messages yet. He's an excellent player – it's just a pity he wasn't born in Barnsley.

> HOWARD WILKINSON, Leeds manager, on his recruit from Nîmes, *1992*.

Journalists arrived from all over Europe to meet him . . . . He gave interviews on art, philosophy and politics. A natural room-mate for David Batty, I thought immediately.

> WILKINSON, in *Managing to Succeed: My Life in Football Management*, with David Walker, *1992*.

You only have to look at my performances for Leeds to be convinced I was worth my place. Eight goals. I was a hit with everyone. I had become the leader.

> CANTONA, by now with Manchester United, looking back on Wilkinson's leaving him out at Leeds, *1993*.

Eric likes to do what he likes, when he likes, because he likes it – and then fuck off. We'd all want a bit of that.

> WILKINSON, *1993*.

It's a funny old game, is it not? One minute I'm thinking, 'Who's that ugly, French, one-eyebrowed git?', then, one trip over the Pennines and suddenly there's this dark, brooding Heathcliff-type figure on the horizon. Not that I'm biased or anything.

> 'LIZEE', Manchester United fan, in article headed 'One for the Ladies' in fanzine *Red Issue, 1993*.

The only English I've heard from him is 'Goal!'

> STEVE BRUCE, Manchester United captain, *1993*.

Tony Cascarino

At Villa I could have gone off for a cup of tea and not been missed.

> CASCARINO, Celtic striker, on his unhappy time at Aston Villa, *1991*.

Lee Chapman

Chappy has that priceless instinct for turning up in the right place at the right time and is so single-minded you sometimes sense his own goal-scoring record is more important to him than anything else in the game.

> HOWARD WILKINSON, Leeds manager, in *Managing to Succeed: My Life in Football Management*, with David Walker, *1992*.

Bobby Charlton

Bobby deserves to keep the record. He was a much better player than me and scored far better goals.

> GARY LINEKER, on retiring from international football one short of Charlton's scoring record for England, *1992.*

They have made Bobby a saint at last.

> GEORGE COHEN, right back in England's World Cup-winning side, on the unveiling of a portrait of Bobby Charlton at the National Portrait Gallery, *1991.*

Nigel Clough

Our No. 9 – the centre-forward.

> BRIAN CLOUGH, Nottingham Forest manager, *1980s.*

He's a playmaker rather than a centre-forward, a better footballer than his old man but not such a good goal-scorer.

> DON HOWE, Queen's Park Rangers coach, *1991.*

They say he doesn't have pace, but he's got the quickest brain you'll ever see in football.

> GRAHAM TAYLOR, England manager, *1992.*

I'm probably one of the slowest front players in the First Division, so beating defenders is a question of making the ball do the work, of being aware of where people are before you get it and then delivering it. Why can Franz Carr run fast and I can't? It's not something I practise. In fact I never really practised any aspect of the game.

> NIGEL CLOUGH, *1991.*

I should have sold him to Terry Venables when I had the chance.

> BRIAN CLOUGH, on how Nigel would have been capped by England earlier had he not spurned Spurs' 1988 approach, *1991.*

The nearest thing to Kenny Dalglish since Dalglish himself stopped playing football.

> GRAEME SOUNESS signing Clough from Forest, *1993.*

Nigel must be a strong character because he played under his father.

> SOUNESS, *1993.*

Charlie Cooke

Charlie Cooke was a winger. He was brilliant. He was a genius. He was as good as George Best and he didn't mess around with women . . . . He ended his career playing for teams called Los Angeles Aztecs, Memphis Rogues and – this one really upsets me – California Surf. I hate to think of him playing on the beach, watched by the cast of *Baywatch*. 'Yo, Charlie!' 'Way to go, Charlie-ie-ie!' Jesus!

> RODDY DOYLE, author of *The Commitments*, on the Chelsea and Scotland winger who was his childhood hero, *1992*.

Gordon 'Sid' Cowans

My ambition is to make a run that Sid doesn't read.

> DAVID PLATT on his link with playmaker Cowans at Aston Villa, *1990*.

Harry Cripps

Before yesterday's game Harry was walking around the dressing room with his fist clenched. 'Come on now, let's have a go. Let's have a go!' . . . We couldn't wait to get out when he had finished. We were almost ready to tear the door down to get out there.

> EAMON DUNPHY, Millwall midfielder, recalling his Cockney captain's motivational powers in his diary of a season, *Only a Game?, 1976*.

In 1991 he was coaching public schoolboys at Winchester.

> RICHARD LINDSAY, author, *Millwall: The Complete Record, 1991*.

I'm surprised myself I landed up here. It's certainly a change from The Den.

> CRIPPS, at Winchester College, *1990*.

Johan Cruyff

We had just watched a video of Johan Cruyff and were to discuss aspects of his play and tactical awareness. Well, this fellow was asked to lead off. What did he think of Cruyff? 'He's a bit greedy.' I couldn't believe it, but it was to get worse. Anything else about him? 'Aye, his left foot's no' as good as his right.' By now the lecturer was giving up, but he thought he'd give the guy one last chance. Anything more you could say about Johan Cruyff? 'He doesnae speak very good English.'

> PAT STANTON, former Scotland player, recalling a coaching course in *The Quiet Man, 1989*.

Tony Daley

He's only got one trick, but it's a good one isn't it?

> GRAHAM TAYLOR, Aston Villa manager, *1989*.

Graham Taylor would have been better off taking Arthur Daley.

> TOMMY DOCHERTY, after-dinner speaker and former manager, after England's unhappy European Championship finals, *1992*.

Kenny Dalglish

Kevin [Keegan] was quicker off the mark, but Kenny runs the first five yards in his head.

BOB PAISLEY on Dalglish's sense of anticipation, *1981*.

I used to think all that stuff about him running the first five yards in his head was rubbish until I'd played with him for a while.

ALAN HANSEN, former Liverpool team-mate, *1992*.

Dion Dublin

Looks a bit like Marvin Hagler, and is even better in the air.

RICHARD WILKINS, Dublin's former team-mate at Cambridge, *1992*.

Dariusz 'Jacki' Dziekanowski

I checked on the 'playboy' image and Billy McNeill, who signed him for Celtic, told me he liked a drink on a Saturday night. I'd be more worried if he stayed in.

JIMMY LUMSDEN, Bristol City manager, on his new Polish striker's reputation, *1992*.

Duncan Edwards

People still haven't forgotten. Strangers come up and tell me: 'He were a good 'un.'

ANNE EDWARDS, 83-year-old mother of the Manchester United and England player who perished 35 years earlier after the Munich air disaster, *1993*.

Justin Fashanu

I wouldn't like to play in the same team as him or even get changed in the vicinity of him.

JOHN FASHANU, Wimbledon striker, on his brother's admission of homosexuality, in BBC TV documentary *Them and Us*, *1991*.

Why should anyone care what happens in my bed? All I've ever said is that I should be judged on my footballing ability.

JUSTIN FASHANU, Torquay striker, *1992*.

I get loads of letters, and not just from gays who think I'm a crusader. I've had no real hate mail, just two complaining when I said in *The Guardian* that I was voting Conservative in the General Election.

JUSTIN FASHANU, *1992*.

Queen of Diamonds

SUN **headline when Fashanu joined Airdrie (nickname 'Diamonds'), *1993*.**

Les Ferdinand

His only fault is his finishing.

> TREVOR BROOKING, TV pundit and ex-international midfielder, on the England striker during 2-0 defeat by Norway, *1993*.

Trevor Francis

I limp better than anyone else and could probably push Trevor Francis close in that area.

> BRIAN ROBERTS, Birmingham defender and *Sports Argus* columnist, *1990*.

Ryan Giggs

One day they might even say I was another Ryan Giggs.

> GEORGE BEST on his latest Manchester United successor, *1992*.

Anyone who tries to talk to Giggs will get a swift kick where it hurts most.

> TERRY YORATH, Wales manager, to media en route to match v Germany in Nuremberg, *1991*. Manchester United also discouraged press attention.

Now I can tell my children that I've played with Ryan Giggs.

> KEVIN RATCLIFFE, veteran Cardiff and Wales defender, after the Welsh victory over Belgium in Giggs' first full international, *1993.*

He just goes out there and gets on with it.

> IAN RUSH, Liverpool and Wales striker, attempting to analyse Giggs' magic, *1993.*

Interviewer: Which song would you like to run out on the pitch to?
Ryan Giggs: 'Wild Thing' by The Troggs.

> MANCHESTER UNITED MAGAZINE, *1993.*

Richard Gough

The ball hit a water sprinkler and shot high into the air. It was purely an instinctive reaction when he grabbed the ball as it flew over his head.

> ANDY ROXBURGH, Scotland coach, on the Rangers captain's sending-off during defeat by Switzerland, *1992.*

Dean Glover

Coolest man alive. Dean is quite easily the best centre-half in the world. Usually takes a book on to the pitch with him to relieve the boredom.

> MEMOIRS OF SETH BOTTOMLEY, Port Vale fanzine, *1989.*

Bruce Grobbelaar

The elastic eccentric.

> JOE LOVEJOY, football correspondent, *The Independent, 1991.*

Perry Groves

A vivid, high-velocity vegetable.

> IVAN PONTING, author, on the carrot-topped striker in *Arsenal Player by Player, 1991.*

Ruud Gullit

I used to see Ruud Gullit play for his first club, Haarlem. We at Ipswich thought he was a promising kid but we felt we had kids like him in England.

> BOBBY ROBSON, PSV Eindhoven manager, *1991.*

They wear caps fitted with the same dreadlocks as me, they have their cars sprayed in the colours of my hair, and write my name on the side. A picture of my face is on every banner. I've pushed this club to the top; I have been the face of AC Milan over the past few years.

> GULLIT, *1992.*

Gheorghe Hagi

He's a brilliant player but we're no' getting all psychedelic about him.

ANDY ROXBURGH, Scotland coach, on the Romanian superstar, *1991*.

John Harkes

He was a bastard on the field. We used to have to tell him, 'We don't like our players head-butting people a whole lot.'

BRUCE ARENA, University of Virginia soccer coach, on Sheffield Wednesday's American midfielder, 1991.

David Hirst

He was a raw youngster with pace and a blistering shot. He had a good attitude but was sometimes very naïve, a trait that earned him the nickname 'Pikey' after the character in *Dad's Army*. Many of his comments were met with the retort 'Stupid boy' in the fashion of Captain Mainwaring.

LEE CHAPMAN, Leeds striker and former Sheffield Wednesday team-mate, in *More Than a Match: A Player's Story, 1992*.

Glenn Hoddle

You didn't have to go up to within 10 yards of him and say, 'Here I am, I want the ball.' You could be a mile away and Hoddle would still find you.

CYRILLE REGIS, Aston Villa striker, regretting that he and Hoddle had not been team-mates, *1992*.

Mark Hughes

A scorer of great goals, but not a great goal-scorer.

DAVID LACEY, football correspondent, *The Guardian, 1989*.

If he has any sense he won't bother coming to Montpellier for the second leg. But being British, no doubt he will come, and I can guarantee that he will get a warm reception.

LUIS NICOLLIN, Montpellier president, before the Cup Winners' Cup quarter-final second leg, *1991*. A French defender had been sent off in the first game after a clash with Hughes.

Roger Hunt

I am proud and privileged to have beaten the record of a great player like Roger Hunt. He was my father's hero. Dad used to call him 'Sir Roger'.

IAN RUSH, overhauling one of Hunt's scoring records for Liverpool, *1992*.

Glenn Hysen

Q: What have Glenn Hysen and Saddam Hussein got in common?
A: They're both lousy in the air.

EVERTONIAN joke during Gulf War, *1991*.

David Icke

It's a Tough Game, Son! – The Real World of Professional Football

TITLE of book by Icke, broadcaster and former Coventry and Hereford goalkeeper, *1983*. Icke later became an environmental campaigner, self-proclaimed prophet and author of *The Truth Vibrations*.

David Icke says he's here to save the world. Well, he saved bugger all when he played for Coventry City.

JASPER CARROTT, comedian, *1992*.

We're more interested in making a profit than signing one.

KEITH NEWBERY, chairman of Newport IOW, on local rivals Ryde's move for Icke, *1991*.

You've Got To Be Crazy

BOB WILSON, goalkeeping book title, *1970s*.

Tommy Johnson

He's brainless and talented, which suits our system.

NEIL WARNOCK, Notts County manager (who later sold the winger to Derby for £1.4 million), *1991*.

Maurice 'Mo' Johnston

I might even agree to become Rangers' first Catholic if they paid me £1 million cash and bought me Stirling Castle . . . . Let me spell out where I stand. I am a Celtic man through and through and so I dislike Rangers because they are a force in Scottish football and therefore a threat to the club I love. But more than that I hate the religious policy they maintain. Why won't they sign a Roman Catholic?

JOHNSTON, Nantes and former Celtic striker, in *Mo: An Autobiography, 1988*.

I'll finish my career here – I don't want to play for any other club.

JOHNSTON on agreeing to rejoin Celtic from the French club, *1989*.

It's a dream! I never thought they'd want me back. I had offers from England and the Continent but I wanted to wear the green and white again. Deep down I've always wanted to be back with Celtic.

> JOHNSTON, after being paraded in a Celtic shirt two months before joining Rangers, *1989*.

I'm just happy to be joining one of the biggest clubs in Europe.

> JOHNSTON on signing for Rangers a few weeks later, *1989*.

He seems to me to be a very brave footballer, facing the wrath of both sets of fans.

> DAVID BRYCE, general secretary, Orange Lodge of Scotland, after Johnston joined Rangers, *1989*.

116 years of tradition ended.

> MESSAGE attached to wreath delivered to Ibrox by Protestant traditionalists, *1989*.

The world of Scottish football was rocked to its pre-cast concrete foundations over the close season when Rangers finally broke with 100 years of tradition and bought a player from FC Nantes for the first time in their history.

> THE ABSOLUTE GAME, Scottish football fanzine, *1989*.

Vinnie Jones

I've been trying to be a footballer and that isn't me. I got a bit carried away with the *Wogan* show and all that.

> JONES, *1990*.

I don't expect Vinnie to do Tony Currie things. Currie couldn't do some of the things Vinnie does.

> DAVE BASSETT, Sheffield United manager, on his new signing from Leeds, *1990*.

I'd like to get 10 goals this season, but the authorities don't normally let me play for a whole season.

> JONES after scoring for United, *1991*.

That's the first time I've been complimented on my passing since handing my UB40 over the counter at the dole office.

> JONES, by now with Chelsea, responding to compliments from former Arsenal captain Frank McLintock, *1991*.

We've got Andy Townsend who leads by example, but Vinnie leads by shaking his fists and that rubs off on other people.

> IAN PORTERFIELD, Chelsea manager, *1991*.

Soccer players have got to be the best controllers of a football, so we thought Vinnie might be able to provide some expertise.

ROSS STRUDWICK, London Crusaders rugby league club coach, on why he had asked Jones to help train his squad, 1992.

If you're going over the top on me you've got to put me out of the game because I'll be coming back for you, whether it's in the next five minutes or next season.

JONES, in *Soccer's Hard Men* video, *1992*.

He is a mosquito brain.

SAM HAMMAM, Wimbledon chairman, after the outrage over Jones's video, *1992*.

Vinnie will be no good to the club, me, man nor beast if he starts acting like Cinderella. We can't have him running around in a tutu and dancing on tiptoes. Vinnie is a hero of the masses. He represents the bulldog spirit of England. He's never set out to maim anyone.

HAMMAM after the FA fined Jones £20,000 and suspended him for six months over the video, *1992*.

As far as I'm concerned, Vinnie is a good role model for children.

JOHN FASHANU, **Wimbledon striker, defending his club-mate, pictured here with young Dons player Vinnie Johns, *1992*.**

At half-time on my Wimbledon debut our old kit-man, Sid, came round with the tea. I asked him how I was doing and he said: 'I'm 85 and if you gave me the No. 4 shirt I'd do better.'

JONES, 1991.

He wouldn't have lasted five minutes in my day.

TOMMY SMITH, former Liverpool hard man, *1992*.

A first-class prat and an embarrassment to football.

SHAUN TEALE, Aston Villa defender, *1992*.

It's about time I grew up.

JONES, after another booking for Wimbledon, *1993*.

We had this sketch suggesting that Vinnie Jones had killed President Kennedy; we had his picture superimposed on a Polaroid of the grassy knoll. The lawyer said: 'You can't do that, it's libel.' Vinnie probably wasn't born, we said, he can't possibly think we mean it. 'Ah', said the lawyer, 'but it's not true, is it? He could sue.' So we didn't do the sketch. I wish we had and Vinnie had sued. It could have been one of the great rulings of English law: *M'lud I refer you to the case of Jones vs TVS and remind you that you cannot say Vinnie Jones killed President Kennedy.*

PAUL MERTON, comedian and comedy writer, recalling TVS programme *Etcetera, 1991*.

Vic Kasule

Baptised 'Vodka Vic' by doting Hamilton Academical fans, [he] will always be remembered at Shrewsbury as the player who overturned a team-mate's car on the way to buy a paper.

STUART COSGROVE, author, *Hampden Babylon: Sex and Scandal in Scottish Football, 1991*.

Roy Keane

He's 19 and he doesn't know where his talent comes from. Nobody does. It's just there.

BRIAN CLOUGH, Nottingham Forest manager, on his £25,000 buy from Irish club Cobh Ramblers, *1991*.

If Keane wants to do that sort of thing, I'll get him a job in a circus.

CLOUGH, on Keane's somersault after scoring the winner in an FA Cup tie at Norwich, *1991*.

The best thing Keane can do is get himself a steady girlfriend and have a courtship. Then he can think about settling down to married life and forget all his frustrations.

> CLOUGH, after a bad-tempered display by the Irishman at Manchester United, *1993*.

He's being a greedy child. He's like a kid who wakes up on Christmas morning and finds an apple, an orange, a box of Smarties and 50p in his stocking. He wants more. Keane is the hottest property in the game right now but he's not going to bankrupt this club.

> CLOUGH on Keane's alleged £6500-a-week wage demands, *1993*.

Brian Kilcline

God knows what was wrong with him. When we get him home, we'll put some scaffolding round him and have a look.

> JOE ROYLE, Oldham manager, on an injury to his man-mountain defender, *1991*.

Jürgen Klinsmann

I've just seen Gary [Lineker] shake hands with Klinsmann – it's a wonder Klinsmann hasn't fallen down.

> RON ATKINSON, ITV pundit, on the German striker's tendency to gamesmanship, World Cup finals, *1990*.

Ronald Koeman

Facing a Koeman free-kick is like facing a serial killer.

> ARCHIE MACPHERSON, TV commentator, during European Championship finals, *1992*.

Oleg Kuznetsov

In principle, I feel all the tasks the manager set me I fulfilled to my own and his satisfaction.

> KUZNETSOV, Ukrainian defender, after his debut for Rangers, *1990*.

Matthew Le Tissier

Ninety per cent of footballers are like racehorses. Useless. Matt is one of the 10 per cent who make it all worthwhile.

> MICK CHANNON, former England striker and racehorse owner, on his Southampton successor, *1992*.

Gary Lineker

Must devote less time to sport if he wants to be a success.

GRAMMAR SCHOOL report on Lineker's final year, when he left with four O Levels, *1970s.*

When you're in the dressing room pulling on your shirt and you look up and see Gary's face, you know you've always got a chance.

PETER SHREEVES, Tottenham manager, *1992.*

It's more like chess than football against him. He's always hiding behind a defender. He never does much until you suddenly realise he's done exactly enough, and by then it's too late.

KENT NIELSEN, Denmark and former Aston Villa defender, *1992.*

[Lineker's legs] are massively thick, silkily muscled pistons of power. They reported back for Tottenham duty at the end of last month. It was enough to make a groupie squawk.

BROUGH SCOTT, sports writer, *Independent on Sunday, 1991.*

Oooh Gary, Gary

FANZINE title, *1990.*

When you think of my record, averaging a goal every two games, it sounds good, but that's only one goal every three hours. Most of the time I am frustrated, pissed off, waiting for the right ball.

LINEKER, *1992.*

It's almost as if Gary is a national institution who cannot be touched. You could argue that we played Brazil with 10 men, but you're not allowed to.

GRAHAM TAYLOR, England manager, after his captain's subdued display v Brazil, *1992.*

I bet one member of my staff £5 that Gary would score twice and break the record tonight and anyone who knows me will know how upset I am about that.

TAYLOR, after Lineker had again failed to score the goal he needed to equal Bobby Charlton's record for England, *1992.*

Gary Who?

NIKE advertising slogan on poster featuring Ian Wright, Lineker's England successor, *1992.*

Lineker 48 Wright 0

QUASER reply on hoardings.

If I'd had Lineker in 1966 I would have played him alongside Geoff Hurst. What a partnership that would have been. They would have fed off each other, and Hurst did so much hard work off the ball he would have dragged defenders all over the place, leaving Lineker free to ply his trade.

> SIR ALF RAMSEY, manager of England's World Cup-winning side, *1992.*

I always score one against the Germans.

> LINEKER, on being dismissed for 1 run batting for the MCC against Germany at Lord's, *1992.*

I'm rather a boring sort of person.

> LINEKER on *Desert Island Discs, 1990.*

The Queen Mother of football.

> DESCRIPTION of Lineker in the play *An Evening with Gary Lineker, 1991.*

One of nature's boy scouts.

> HUNTER DAVIES, feature writer, *The Independent, 1992.*

All that goody-goody stuff gets a bit sickly at times. It can be embarrassing. Nobody is that nice. I know what I'm like, and my family know. I suppose that's all that matters.

> LINEKER, asked about his 'squeaky-clean' image, *1992.*

I do swear, you know. In fact, I swore only the other week. The lads are always saying, 'Ooh , we're telling on you, Gary Lineker swore.'

> LINEKER, *1992.*

I aim to play more cricket, go to the Olympics, take two family holidays, go to the Open golf and, oh yes, keep myself fit.

> LINEKER on his plans between leaving Spurs and moving to Japan, *1992.*

David Lowe

After hearing our striker David Lowe on the radio the other day, my sister was wondering if he does the voice-over for the turtle on the electricity ads.

> LETTER to *The Fox*, Leicester fanzine, *1993.*

James Major

MAJOR MINOR'S A MINI VINNIE!

DAILY STAR headline after Major, son of the Prime Minister, was sent off for the fourth time in a season playing for his public school, Kimbolton, *1993*.

If he wants to play dirty he should follow his old man into politics.

TOMMY SMITH, former Liverpool hard man, *1993*.

I'm sure the lad will learn. He shouldn't worry about it too much. Tell the kid not to lose his passion, no matter who his dad is.

VINNIE JONES after Major Jnr's dismissal for 'violent conduct', *1993*.

Diego Maradona

I can't be sure I won't do the same again because in the heat of a game, your hand goes off on its own.

MARADONA after referee had failed to spot his handling a shot in Argentina v Soviet Union match, World Cup finals, *1990*.

The information we have is that the player was intoxicated with drugs and just asked to be allowed to sleep.

JULIO MERA FIGUEROA, Argentina's Minister of the Interior, announcing that Maradona had been arrested for drug possession, *1991*.

I want to die! I want to die! I can't take any more. My God, get me out of here!

MARADONA, in his Buenos Aires jail cell, according to *Cronica* newspaper, *1991*.

Maradona is finished – don't lynch him.

L'UNITA newspaper headline, Italy, *1991*.

He's a poor, sick boy who must be helped to rid himself of this vice which is destroying him morally and materially.

CARLOS MENEM, President of Argentina, *1991*.

We're looking for players who are role models not parole models.

KENNY COOPER, coach of American club Baltimore Blast, on reports that he was to sign Maradona, *1992*.

Now I am number 10,000, but let me fight on the field to get back to what I was. Then you can judge if I'm No. 10,000 or No. 1.

MARADONA, signing for Seville after his 18-month ban, *1992*.

Gary Mabbutt

I'm the Marjorie Proops of diabetes.

MABBUTT, Spurs' diabetic captain, on his heavy postbag, *1992.*

Sir Stanley Matthews

His name is symbolic of the beauty of the game, his fame timeless. A magical player, of the people, for the people.

INSCRIPTION on statue of Matthews in Hanley, his birthplace, *1987.*

The maestro appears to be dribbling towards Millett's but could easily swerve across the street to Woolworth's.

GUINNESS FOOTBALL ENCYCLOPEDIA, ed. Graham Hart, describing the statue, *1991.*

I'm still light on my feet. I feel I could run across quicksand.

SIR STAN, self-confessed fitness freak, at 76, *1991.*

Gary McAllister

I thought Edith Piaf had the franchise on singing 'No Regrets', but I think I've heard it more times from McAllister in the last six months. I just wish he'd stop talking about me. I can only assume I upset him when we met because he was wearing cowboy boots and I asked if he was related to John Wayne.

BRIAN CLOUGH, Nottingham Forest manager, on the Scottish international who turned down Forest before joining Leeds, *1991.*

Frank McAvennie

Whilst the rest of Scotland's footballing anti-heroes stumbled from one seedy den to another, drinking everything in their way, Frank McAvennie has devoted his life to human affection. In the words of one over-excited Fleet Street commentator, 'his tipple is nipple'.

STUART COSGROVE, author, in *Hampden Babylon: Sex and Scandal in Scottish Football, 1991.*

Ally McCoist

I was thrilled until I learned that Ivan Lendl had finished above me.

ALLY MCCOIST, Rangers and Scotland striker, on being named fifth best-looking sportsman in the world, *1990.*

He's handsome, he's rich, he's funny and he's happy – my envy knows no bounds.

BILLY CONNOLLY, comedian, in foreword to *Ally McCoist: My Story, 1992.*

Paul McGrath

Ooh, Aah, Paul McGrath.

> DUBLIN CROWD rap-style chant on Republic of Ireland's homecoming after World Cup finals, *1990.*

Ooh, Aah, Paul McGrath's Da.

> DUBLIN CROWD later the same day, greeting Nelson Mandela.

Popular opinion seems to have it that after he moved to Aston Villa, Graham Taylor found the right way to handle him, giving him a professional minder, more medical help and the like. I must tell you, we offered him every facility and advice we could think of. Sir Matt Busby spoke to him along with the club doctor, Francis McHugh, and we even got his parish priest in to try and help.

> ALEX FERGUSON, Manchester United manager, in *Six Years at United, 1992.*

The best defender in the world, bar none.

> RON ATKINSON, Villa manager, *1993.*

Just think how good he'd be with two good knees.

> KEVIN RICHARDSON, Villa captain, *1993.*

Steve McManaman

We've another boy who's 10 and if he sees a tin can on his way to school, he steps over it. Steven was the opposite.

> DAVID MCMANAMAN, father of the Liverpool winger, *1991.*

Paul McStay

Stamina: I should give him 12 out of 10, but I'm not really an expert on the subject.

> JIM BAXTER, former Rangers and Scotland midfielder, evaluating the Celtic captain's strengths, *1992.*

McStay for Rangers? Sounds like a fair swap to me.

> LETTER to *Sunday Mail* after speculation that the play-maker might move to Ibrox, *1992.*

Ludek Miklosko

You are continually going up for the ball and finding he's taken it off your head. Which makes a nice change at West Ham.

> TONY GALE, West Ham defender, on his club's 6 ft 4 in Czechoslovak 'keeper, *1991.*

To add to West Ham's anxiety Miklosko, their tree-trunk of a goalkeeper, is displaying symptoms of Czech elm disease.

> DAVID LACEY, football correspondent, *The Guardian, 1991.*

Roger Milla

We are very pleased Roger unretired.

> VALERI NEPOMNIACHI, Cameroon's Russian coach, on his ageless striker at World Cup finals, *1990.*

I was already an international superstar before the World Cup. It was just that the Europeans didn't recognise it.

> MILLA, *1991.*

My age doesn't matter. How old was your Stanley Matthews when he retired?

> MILLA, declining to divulge his age before England v Cameroon friendly, *1991.* A year later he played against South Africa, reputedly aged 40.

Willie Miller

If we had rugby union's 10-metre rule in our game, Willie Miller of Aberdeen would have played most of his football in Norway.

> TONY HIGGINS, Scottish Professional Footballers' Association chairman, *1991.*

Jan Molby

Molby looked corpulent enough to be playing darts for Denmark.

> BRIAN GLANVILLE, football correspondent, *The Sunday Times, 1985.*

Beneath the drayman's body, his feet remain as nimble as a ballet dancer's.

> HUGH MCILVANNEY, sports writer, *The Observer*, reporting Liverpool v Leeds match at which the visiting fans chanted 'Sumo' at the midfielder, *1992.*

Bobby Moore

There should be a law against him. He knows what's happening 20 minutes before anybody else.

> JOCK STEIN, Celtic manager, *1960s.*

The greatest defender I have ever faced.

PELE, after Brazil v England match at World Cup finals, Mexico, *1970*.

Opposing managers and players were always looking for weaknesses in Moore's armoury. They discovered so many – lack of speed, poor heading ability, and lack of venom in the tackle – that it was a wonder he ever progressed beyond the local park. Poor chaps: they had missed the essence of Moore's game. His most important asset was the quickness of his mind, and the vision to assess a situation before others had noticed the situation existed.

BRYON BUTLER, journalist, *Daily Telegraph* after Moore's death, *1993*.

He was the heartbeat of the team in 1966. He was my right-hand man, my lieutenant on the field, a cool, calculating footballer I could trust with my life.

SIR ALF RAMSEY, former England manager, leading tributes to his former captain, *1993*.

To find a way past him was like searching for the exit from Hampton Court Maze.

DAVID MILLER, journalist, *The Times, 1993*.

Stan Mortensen

They'll probably call it the Matthews funeral.

GUARDIAN journalist after Mortensen's death, *1991*.

Jackie Mudie

You could sum up his ability in three words: skill, skill and skill.

TONY WADDINGTON, former Stoke City manager, on the death of Stanley Matthews' ex-inside-forward partner, *1992*.

Andy Murdoch

Andy has an answerphone installed on his six-yard line and the message says: 'Sorry I'm not in just now, but if you'd like to leave the ball in the back of the net I'll get back to you as soon as I can.'

JIM DUFFY, Partick Thistle captain, writing about his goalkeeper in the club programme, *1991*.

Charlie Nicholas

I was blessed in those days but Arsenal took it away from me. They would fire it forward, but I've never had the pace to get away from defenders. My game's about thinking faster, not running faster.

NICHOLAS, Aberdeen striker, lamenting his Highbury sojourn, *1990*.

Scott Nisbet

Every pass an adventure.

WALTER SMITH, Rangers manager, on Ibrox cult figure Nisbet, *1993*.

Carlton Palmer

He's the worst finisher since Devon Loch. When he's in a clear shooting position he's under orders to do just one thing – pass.

RON ATKINSON, Sheffield Wednesday manager, *1991*.

Darko Pancev

I can't dribble, I can't pass, but I'm the best striker in Europe.

PANCEV, Red Star Belgrade striker, on winning the Golden Boot as Europe's top scorer, *1991*.

Jean-Pierre Papin

I have spoken to Eric Cantona several times about Papin and have been left in little doubt about his single-mindedness. He rarely goes out to socialise but instead stays at home to watch his vast library of goal videos.

> LEE CHAPMAN, Leeds striker, *1992*.

Paul Parker

The little lad jumped like a salmon and tackled like a ferret.

> BOBBY ROBSON, England manager, at World Cup finals, *1990*.

Stuart Pearce

I went to have a look at him playing for Wealdstone on a stinking night at Yeovil. After eight minutes he put in a thundering tackle and the Yeovil winger landed in my wife's lap. I said to her: 'That's it. I've seen enough. We're going home.'

> BOBBY GOULD, West Brom manager, recalling signing Pearce for Coventry, *1991*.

Pearce captained Forest but he has a reluctance to talk to the press, and there is a responsibility to converse with the media.

> GRAHAM TAYLOR, England manager, on why he initially overlooked Pearce's claim to succeed Bryan Robson as captain, *1990*.

The London press (you know, the ones Pearcey won't talk to) . . . .

> BRIAN CLOUGH, Nottingham Forest manager, programme column, *1990*.

When you look him in the eye you get total honesty.

> TAYLOR, on changing his mind and naming Pearce to succeed Gary Lineker as captain, *1992*.

Pele

He was unselfish, a true team man. He was playing with blokes who'd spent their careers with Watford and Sheffield United, but he never thought himself above them.

> STEVE HUNT, former New York Cosmos team-mate, on the great Brazilian's 50th birthday, *1990*.

Michel Platini

I have some very bad news for you – Platini's just retired.

> ISLAMIC hostage-taker to Frenchman Roger Auque in film *Hors la Vie*, based on his real-life captivity in 1987 in Beirut, *1992*.

David Platt

When I hit the pillow the one player I never worry about is David Platt.

GRAHAM TAYLOR, England manager, *1992*.

His product continually exceeds his talent.

TAYLOR, *1992*.

He was not exceptional at anything, but pretty good at everything.

DARIO GRADI, Crewe manager, on the player he recruited free from Manchester United, *1992*.

I took my wife to watch him play for Crewe at Newport one Christmas. In the second half he volleyed a pass to his own goalkeeper and then, when a cross came in at the other end a matter of seconds later, Platt made the header. Everyone saw the header, but it was the 90-yard run that went unseen, and that is what I found impressive.

TAYLOR, recalling the 'unseen work' that prompted him to buy Platt for Aston Villa, *1990*.

If Georgie Best is the Keith Richards of football, Platt is the Paul McCartney: keen, clean and a real pro, but not quite the lily-white goody-goody.

ED VULLIAMY, *Guardian* reporter, after Platt's £5.5 million move from Villa to Bari, *1991*.

David is not as good as Maradona but he is more of a team player and that is why we paid £5.5 million for him. I also believe he is a more complete player than Paul Gascoigne.

VINCENZO MATTARESE, Bari president, *1991*.

When he came back from Italy for the friendly with Germany he wanted to open the batting, open the bowling, keep wicket, field at first slip and take catches on the boundary all at the same time.

TAYLOR, on Platt's first match for England after his move to Italy, *1991*.

As far as I'm concerned, for nine months of the year I am no longer English. When I am with Bari I am an Italian. I want to speak Italian, dress Italian, eat Italian and live Italian.

PLATT, *1991*.

Mick Quinn

He's the football equivalent of Polaris when the ball lands in the penalty area. Up comes his periscope and suddenly there is a submarine on the surface of the water and the missile has been fired. Opponents don't realise he's there until it's too late – and they are holed below the Plimsoll line.

BOBBY GOULD, Coventry manager, on his widely travelled striker, *1993*.

Cyrille Regis

I know Cyrille's found God. Now I want him to find the devil.

RON ATKINSON, Aston Villa manager, *1992*.

Peter Reid

It's like *Star Trek*. He boldly goes where no man has gone before.

HOWARD KENDALL, Manchester City manager, *1990*.

At QPR his legs looked all right, but the hooped strip didn't do him any favours.

KENDALL, *1990*.

Frank Rijkaard

If he'd have done it to me, I'd have chinned him.

JACK CHARLTON, Republic of Ireland manager, on Rijkaard–Rudi Völler spitting incident, World Cup finals, *1990*.

Mark Robins

The boy just comes alive in the box. Nine-tenths of what Mark Hughes does is fantastic, but Robins possesses the other tenth.

ALEX FERGUSON, Manchester United manager, two years before selling Robins to Norwich, *1990*.

John Robertson

He was a very unattractive young man. If ever I felt off colour I'd sit next to him, because compared with this fat, dumpy lad I was Errol Flynn. But give him a ball and a yard of grass and he was an artist.

BRIAN CLOUGH, Nottingham Forest manager, on his former winger in the video *Cloughie*, *1990*.

Bryan Robson

Lesser players have won more but none has given as much.

> BOBBY ROBSON, former England manager, *1990*.

England were a taller, prouder team when he played.

> BOBBY ROBSON, *1991*.

The best half-backs ever were Duncan Edwards and Dave Mackay. Robbo is right there with them.

> RON ATKINSON, Robson's manager at West Brom and Manchester United, *1991*.

I look for two things in a player. Skill and attitude – side by side, not one above the other. And Robson has been the outstanding example for 10 years.

> GEORGE GRAHAM, Arsenal manager, *1990*.

Some said his bravery bordered on stupidity, but without that courage he would have been just another good player.

> BOBBY ROBSON, in *Against All Odds, 1990*.

He is three players in one, a defender, a midfielder and a phemonenal goal-scorer. He was dominant in set-plays at both ends. Maybe I'm biased but I could see no failings. Off the field, maybe, but never on it.

> BOBBY ROBSON, as above.

Maybe he's not a great player any more, but he's a great coach. He tells the others where to play.

> WIM SUVRIJN, Montpellier player, after United's Cup Winners' Cup victory over the French club, *1991*.

Ian Rush

There's been a long history between Liverpool and Ian Rush. It's been a great love affair, and now it can carry on.

> PETER ROBINSON, Liverpool chief executive, as the Welshman signed a new, long-term contract, *1992*.

Hugo Sanchez

He is a very dangerous man, as welcome as a piranha fish in a bidet.

> JESUS GIL, Atletico Madrid president, on Real Madrid's Mexican striker, *1992*.

Dean Saunders

Deano makes you feel anything is possible. Given the choice, most of us would sooner buy Saunders than Gazza.

> NEVILLE SOUTHALL, Wales goalkeeper, *1990*.

He's a boy who needs encouragement. He's had that in the past, but it doesn't work like that at Liverpool. You're told it's time to grow up.

> GRAEME SOUNESS, Liverpool manager, as his £2.9 million striker struggled for form at Anfield, *1991*.

If I'd had him with the group I had at Manchester United – the Robsons, Strachans, Olsens and Stapletons – we'd have won everything going, including the Ashes. He's the best natural finisher I've ever worked with.

> RON ATKINSON, **Aston Villa manager, on his £2.3 million recruit,** *1992.*

Dean Saunders says he's finding it difficult without John Barnes. He should try playing at the bottom of the Fourth Division.

MICKEY THOMAS, Wrexham captain, 1992.

Being constantly criticised at Liverpool wore me down. I'm someone who needs to be loved.

SAUNDERS, after joining Aston Villa, 1992.

It's no good buying someone and then telling them they're crap. You have to know your product. At Liverpool, Dean has been going into areas where he can't score goals. He's at his best when he's running on the ball and getting to the byline. Last night we gave him a rollicking because he was starting to run away from goal to look for the ball. That's no good for us.

TERRY YORATH, Wales manager, 1992.

Peter Schmeichel

People say we have the best goalkeeper in the world. I wonder why we didn't bring him.

FLEMING POVLSEN, Denmark striker, after the Manchester United 'keeper's tentative start to the European Championship finals, 1992.

David Seaman

I have been in the game for years, written books, made videos and coached on goalkeeping. But in my 50th year, I still find I am being taught things by David Seaman. That's how good I think he is.

BOB WILSON, former Arsenal and Scotland goalkeeper and TV pundit, 1991.

'And David Seaman will be very disappointed about that'

TITLE of pop single by The Lillywhites, taken from TV commentary when the Arsenal 'keeper was beaten by Gary Lineker in the FA Cup semi-final, 1991.

Lee Sharpe

The first time I saw him I felt a bit like the bloke who discovered George Best. He scored inside five minutes, and then he scored again. And he was still at school.

JOHN JAMES, Torquay chief scout, on spotting the Manchester United winger in the Black Country, 1991.

He had so much class he unsettled my stomach.

CYRIL KNOWLES, Sharpe's manager at Torquay, 1989.

Lee is about 20 times better looking than Gazza.

> COMPANY, women's magazine, article on 'Britain's 50 Most Eligible Bachelors', *1992*.

You won't find him living it up in discos and clubs.

> THE PEOPLE, magazine section, 10 May, *1992*.

Manchester United kids Lee Sharpe and Ryan Giggs have been fined a staggering £14,000 . . . . Sharpe, 21, and Giggs, 18, disobeyed the order and took off to Blackpool where they spent a night on the town.

> THE PEOPLE, sports section, 10 May, *1992*.

Alan Shearer

The lad's in a class of his own. Only 22, but already a man. Dean Saunders scores goals as well, but his head can drop. Shearer lifts the entire team, turns draws into victories. Priceless.

> KENNY DALGLISH, Blackburn manager, on his £3.3 million striker, *1992*.

I never believed any footballer was worth £3.3 million until I saw Shearer playing for Blackburn.

> ALAN HANSEN, former Liverpool captain and TV football analyst, *1992*.

A person you'd be delighted to have as your son.

> KENNY DALGLISH, Blackburn manager, *1992*.

He is the perfect all-round leader of the line and leader of the team. He has inspired the whole team, he has made players you saw struggling in last season's Second Division bubble in the Premier League.

> GORDON TAYLOR, PFA chief executive and Blackburn fan, *1992*

People keep talking about the money, but just look at what we've go. He is a wonderful player. He will be one of the great Blackburn players to compare with anything we have had before.

> JACK WALKER, Blackburn's multi-millonaire backer, *1992*.

Peter Shilton

Shilton criticises himself for leaking goals that the combined talents of Clemence, Banks, Southall and Grobbelaar in the same net couldn't keep out.

> JOHN BARNES, England team-mate, after Shilton was beaten by a long-range shot v Uruguay, *1990*.

Craig Short

I'm not sure how I became worth an extra £1 million in the space of two months without kicking a ball. Mind you, I did get married in the summer and looked quite impressive on the beach during my honeymoon.

> CRAIG SHORT, Derby defender, on moving from Notts County for £2.5 million after earlier being valued at £1.5 million, *1992.*

Jan Stejskal

He only knows three words of English – 'My ball', 'Away!' and one other.

> RAY WILKINS, QPR midfielder, on his club's Czechoslovak goalkeeper, *1991.*

Gordon Strachan

You could video that and sell it as what you expect from a player – the control, the passing, the will to take responsibility, to work to retrieve situations. Gordon defends better than some people twice as big as him, twice as strong and twice as athletic.

> HOWARD WILKINSON, Leeds manager, *1992.*

When I was a teenager at Dundee and I saw the senior players I used to think, 'Well, if I'm with Arbroath at that age, getting £30 a week and all the kippers I can eat, I'll be doing pretty well for myself.'

> STRACHAN, captaining Leeds at 33, *1990.*

It's a tremendous honour – I'm going to have a banana to celebrate.

> STRACHAN, on being voted football writers' Footballer of the Year, *1991.*

He's got one of these gurus to sort out his diet – me, I just eat owt.

> DAVID BATTY, Leeds team-mate, on Strachan's bananas-and-seaweed pills regime, in *An Alternative History of Leeds United, 1991.*

Last Wednesday, Strachan set about Oldham like a one-man swarm. Some even felt Leeds's first goal should be regarded as unofficial since it didn't involve him. Never fear, he set up the second which clinched the tie.

> KEVIN MCCARRA, football correspondent, *Scotland on Sunday, 1990.*

For a man so small in size he's a person of great stature who can destroy at once the big tough guys in the dressing room with one lash of his coruscating tongue. That's why he earned the nickname 'King Tongue'.

> WILKINSON, in *Managing to Succeed: My Life in Football Management*, with David Walker, *1992.*

Geoff Thomas

Isn't he the one who can trap a ball as far as I used to be able to kick it?

> GEORGE BEST, on the Crystal Palace and England midfielder, *1993*.

Mickey Thomas

I'm the Cliff Richard of football.

> THOMAS, 37-year-old former Wales midfielder, before scoring Wrexham's winner in FA Cup v Arsenal, *1992*.

Brian Flynn: If he was 10 years younger he would be worth £5 million.
Thomas: Is that all?

> EXCHANGE between player-manager and match-winner after Arsenal tie.

Simon Tracey

He's got the brains of a rocking horse.

> DAVE BASSETT, Sheffield United manager, after his 'keeper's sending-off at Spurs, *1992*.

Marco van Basten

He's got everything: quick, strong, good in the air, powerful in his shooting from long or short range, and yet creative. In other words, complete.

> GARY LINEKER, *1992*.

Chris Waddle

I'm fed up with dribbling showmen like Waddle. One is enough. Now he can stay out of the way on the wing.

> BERNARD TAPIE, Marseille president, after signing Trevor Steven, *1991*.

Le roi du déhanchement . . . le magicien du ballon rond, il est tout cela. (The king of swaying hips . . . the magician of the round ball, he is all these things.)

> ADVERTISING blurb for French video *Chris Magic Waddle, 1993*.

It's certainly a long way from the sausage factory.

> WADDLE, recalling his first job in the North-East as Sheffield Wednesday prepared for third trip to Wembley in quick succession, *1993*.

Des Walker

You'll never beat Des Walker.

> FOREST fans' chant, *1990s*.

You'll never meet Des Walker.

> JOURNALISTS' joke, *1990*. Walker never talked to the press during his time at Forest.

Journalists talk in hushed tones about the times Des said to them: 'No comment.' That other thoroughbred Dessie, Orchid of that ilk, has been more forthcoming in the past.

> ANDY COLQUHOUN, football correspondent, *Birmingham Post, 1992*.

I'm a defender and not a goal-scorer, and for the first few years of my career no one wanted interviews. After that I decided not to put any pressure on myself.

> WALKER, breaking his silence, *1992*.

He'll be back for another interview in 10 years.

> LAWRIE MCMENEMY, England assistant manager, after rare Walker interview, *1992*.

England's hidden sweeper.

> SEPP PIONTEK, Turkey manager, on Walker's tendency to intercept rather than tackle, *1992*.

Neil Webb

He's not actually a very good player but he's got a lovely smile that brightens up Monday mornings.

> BRIAN CLOUGH, Nottingham Forest manager, on why he was considering buying Webb back from Manchester United, *1991*.

Norman Whiteside

If [Chris] Waddle cost £4 million, Norman must be worth £9 million.

> TOMMY DOCHERTY, former Manchester United manager, after Whiteside's £250,000 transfer from United to Everton, *1989*.

Frank Worthington

He will go on playing until he can't walk.

> BILLY LEGG, manager of non-league Guiseley, for whom Worthington was turning out in his 40s, *1990*.

I had 11 clubs – 12 if you count Stringfellows.

> WORTHINGTON, former England striker, *1993*.

Ian Wright

As a person, Ian is quite disciplined. It's just that once that whistle goes, he still plays football the way he has played it since his non-League days. Bursting to win. If you were to take away that edge, you'd lose the exciting player that was. I don't think Ian can play in control. He's intuitive and instinctive – make him think and the intuition is lost.

GEORGE GRAHAM, Arsenal manager, on his volatile striker, *1993*.

He's almost uncoachable, so I can't claim any credit.

GRAHAM, after more Wright goals, *1993*.

I'm not dirty or malicious. This thing is getting out of control. I didn't touch [Alan] McDonald and I don't believe I deserved to get booked.

WRIGHT, getting his seventh booking of the season in January for a challenge which broke three of the QPR defender's ribs, *1992*.

On his first day at Palace he told me he wanted to play for England, which was quite a bold statement for someone who'd just walked in off a building site.

STEVE COPPELL, Crystal Palace manager, *1993*.

Mark Wright

He'd get an injury even if he went on *Question of Sport*.

TOMMY DOCHERTY, after-dinner speaker and former manager, *1992*.

Dwight Yorke

If that lad makes a First Division footballer, my name is Mao Tse Tung.

TOMMY DOCHERTY, former Villa manager, on the club's 'frightened' newcomer, *1991*. The Trinidadian striker finished the following season as top scorer.

TEAMS AND CLUBS

Airdrieonians

We ended up playing football, and that doesn't suit our style.

ALEX MACDONALD, Airdrie manager, after defeat at Aberdeen, *1991*.

Aldershot

Things are dire. Paramount is the payment of Christmas wages. We haven't even got a Christmas card. All the other clubs send Christmas cards. We haven't got one.

STEVE BIRLEY, club secretary, *1991*.

This is life in the shadow of the Premier League. The financial situation is hopeless and people are beating our door down demanding their money.

BIRLEY, as Aldershot's demise came closer, *1992*.

Arsenal

We were left counting our bruises. It's not what you expect in what is basically a friendly.

> ROBERTO MANCINI, Sampdoria striker, after playing Arsenal in Makita Tournament, *1990*.

I'm very impressed. They are super.

> JOHN MAJOR, Prime Minister, after watching the 5–0 defeat of Aston Villa at Highbury, *1991*.

Arsenal remind me of the army a little bit – a group of highly trained professionals who can so easily step over the line into illegality. They are simply too close to the edge.

> DUNCAN MCKENZIE, former player and *Today* columnist, after a mass brawl against Manchester United, *1990*.

These incidents have sullied the name of Arsenal Football Club. It is not a tradition of this club to have a bad reputation.

> PETER HILL-WOOD, Arsenal chairman, fining manager George Graham and the players for Old Trafford fracas, *1990*.

They were all shouting at each other. It was all 'f' this and 'f' that. I stepped in to calm things down, otherwise I'm sure punches would have been thrown.

> DION DUBLIN, striker with Third Division Cambridge, after Arsenal players squared up to each other during FA Cup tie, *1991*.

I like to see that sort of thing. It's just a bit of passion on the pitch – players geeing one another up. In the past we've heard so much about southern softies, but we have the character and desire of any northern team. It's one of the qualities of being successful.

> GEORGE GRAHAM, Arsenal manager, after Cambridge tie.

[Alan] Smith and [Kevin] Campbell are looking formidable. With [Anders] Limpar and [Paul] Merson on the flanks I get excited when I put their names on the team-sheet.

> GRAHAM, as his side closed on the League title, *1991*.

People say Arsenal lack flair, but it is there. It's just camouflaged by the fact that they have a strict discipline. Because they don't concede goals doesn't mean they don't have flair.

> ALEX FERGUSON, Manchester United manager, *1991*.

Boring, boring Arsenal.

> ARSENAL fans, adopting opposition supporters' chant as their team romped to the Championship, *1991*.

Barnet

We drink beer and swear a lot at each other.

> BARRY FRY, manager, on Barnet's arrival in the Fourth Division, *1991*.

We can go through the divisions like Wimbledon, but with more style.

> MARK CARTER, Barnet striker, *1991*.

Barnet has been a big part of my life. I took a second mortgage to save them. I gave them my testimonial money. I got arrested driving the tractor on Christmas Day to flatten the pitch, and when I said I was the manager the policeman said, 'Oh yes, and I'm George Best.'

> FRY, after leaving Barnet for Southend, *1993*.

Being manager of Barnet was like living with a double-decker bus on your head. When I left it was like it had been driven off. I was meeting with the FA, then the Football League, then solicitors, then councillors, the PFA, the players, people trying to buy the club. Life was one big meeting.

> FRY, recalling troubled times at Barnet, *1993*.

Blackburn Rovers

The way we've gone we make Manchester United look cheap.

> JACK WALKER, Blackburn president and multi-millionaire backer, on Kenny Dalglish's spending spree, *1992*.

I had to read the papers to find out who we were buying next.

> TONY PARKES, Blackburn assistant manager, *1991*.

If they have got a weakness they just go out and buy the best player and plug it.

> MIKE WALKER, Norwich manager, *1992*.

We're fortunate to have a half-decent squad.

> KENNY DALGLISH, Blackburn manager, after spending £13 million on players, *1992*.

Cambridge United

We want to provide thrills with no frills. That isn't easy for a Cockney like me to say.

> JOHN BECK, Cambridge manager, as team were criticised for long-ball approach and gamesmanship, *1991*.

It's not the players' idea of fun, but the cold showers seem to wake us up.

> DION DUBLIN, Cambridge striker, on Beck's imposition of compulsory cold showers before matches, *1990*.

Primitive and robotic – and that's being kind. It's worse than Wimbledon in their early days.

> NEIL WEBB, Manchester United midfielder, after League Cup tie, *1991*.

This isn't football, it's war games.

> RICHARD MURRAY, Charlton director, *1991*.

By the end of the game even their own fans were chanting: 'We want football.'

> DUNCAN SHEARER, Swindon striker, after FA Cup win over Beck's team, *1992*.

When we got to the dressing room there were two big plates of biscuits and all the morning papers, put there to deliberately wind us up. They were thinking we'd sit down, relax and forget about the game . . . Out on the pitch they're just as bad. They sand the four corners so that the ball holds up when they punt it into those areas, and when we played them at the start of the season they left the grass really long so that passing was difficult.

> SHEARER, as above.

A player shouted 'to feet' in training and was punished by being made to do 40 press-ups.

> STEVE CLARIDGE, striker, on leaving Cambridge for Luton, *1992*.

When you don't enjoy a single training session, it's time to go.

> COLIN BAILLIE, former Cambridge captain, *1992*.

Cameroon

When an African team takes part in a tournament like this, the players are always asked two questions by foreign journalists: 'Do you have a witch doctor?' and 'Do you eat monkeys?'

> FRANÇOIS OMAM BIYICK, Cameroon player, World Cup finals, *1990*.

We didn't underestimate them. They were a lot better than we thought.

> BOBBY ROBSON, England manager, after 3–2 victory over Cameroon, World Cup finals, *1990*.

I was happy because they could go with their heads high as they did throughout the World Cup, even when they had all those red cards. They just play with their hearts, they don't go out there to kill. The player's kicked out of the match, but he still goes out with a smile and a wave to the crowd. He didn't mean to hurt anybody – he just didn't want the guy to pass by.

> CHARLIE NTAMARK, Walsall and former Cameroon player, recalling his country's exit from the 1990 World Cup finals, *1991*.

Our style of play will never change because we never had one in the first place. We just do whatever comes into our heads.

> NTAMARK, when the Africans came to Wembley, *1991*.

Celtic

We don't just want to win this cup. We want to win by playing good football, to make neutrals glad we won it.

> JOCK STEIN, Celtic manager, before victory in European Cup final over Inter Milan, *1967*.

I only know the first two lines of 'The Sash' because after that we've usually scored.

> ROY AITKEN, Celtic captain, on the age-old rivalry with Rangers, *1980s*.

Hibs 1, Celtic – they must be getting used to it – 0.

> SIR ALISTAIR BURNET, reading the results on ITV's *News at Ten, 1990*.

Crystal Palace

When we try to play nice football we don't do very well.

> ALAN SMITH, Palace assistant manager, on his club's 'direct' style, *1990*.

You don't want a date with your wife or girlfriend after playing Palace. It would be difficult to kiss them without smooth lips.

> HOWARD KENDALL, Everton manager, *1991*.

It's a man's game and men make tackles and I hope men accept tackles without bleating too much.

> STEVE COPPELL, Palace manager, after robust game against Sheffield United, *1991*.

If that's what football is about, then I'll have to look for another job.

> GRAEME SOUNESS, Liverpool manager, after a 1–1 League Cup draw with Palace, *1992*.

Denmark

I've told Chancellor Kohl that it is absolutely not on for the Danes to want to leave the European Community and, at the same time, be European champions.

> BERTI VOGTS, Germany coach, before the European Championship Final – won 2–0 by the Danes – in Gothenburg, *1992*.

Journalist: Have you had a few beers?
Fleming Poulsen: No – we have had a lot of beers.

> EXCHANGE at press conference after Denmark reached the Final, *1992*.

The Danes were all over the place – there wasn't any order.

> GUIDO BUCHWALD, **Germany defender, as Denmark celebrated (below).**

A month ago I was on my summer holidays. Now we're the European champions. It takes some getting used to.

> PETER SCHMEICHEL, Manchester United and Denmark goalkeeper, on his country's triumph in the European finals as late replacements for Yugoslavia.

I never thought about reaching the Final before this tournament started. My brain wasn't big enough to think that far ahead.

> RICHARD MÖLLER NIELSEN, Denmark coach, after the Final.

Denmark showed that football is also about fighting. To dominate the game you have to win the battles and we were losing most of them in the first half.

> RINUS MICHELS, Holland coach, after Denmark defeated the favourites in the semi-final.

Derby County

What a year – war in the Gulf, economic recession, and Derby County relegated.

> ANDREW WARD, ANTON RIPPON and GERALD MORTIMER, authors, *The Derby County Story, 1991.*

Egypt

Interviewer: Jack, which of the Egyptians has impressed you?
Jack Charlton: I couldn't tell you, I don't know their names. There was the boy with the beard, the dark lad in midfield, the 'keeper, the little dark lad who played centre-midfield, the very coloured boy and the boy who played up front – Hassan, Hussain?

> EXCHANGE at Republic of Ireland press conference, World Cup finals, *1990.*

England 1966

I'd have preferred it if neither team had reached the Final. I'm not a great lover of the Germans – they bombed my folks' house in Clydebank during the war.

> ALLY MACLEOD, former Scotland manager, on 25th anniversary of England v West Germany Final, *1991.*

I was on a boat to Campbeltown at the time and, even though I was listening to it on the radio, I was convinced the third goal had not crossed the line . . . England are the first country to win the World Cup 2–2. It was a black day.

> ALEX SALMOND, Scottish Nationalist Party leader, *1991.*

For the sake of peace and quiet, we hope England win no other sporting event until at least the middle of the next century. And that even then, it's only the world whist championship.

> SUN leader article, Scottish edition only, *1991.*

It never crossed our minds that we could lose. No, no never. It didn't come into it.

> BOBBY MOORE, captain of England's World Cup-winning team, in Ian Ridley, *Season in the Cold : A Journey Through English Football, 1992.*

England 1992

English football is committing suicide through the length of its domestic season. Their players arrive burnt out. They will be hard pressed to reach the semi-finals.

> FRANZ BECKENBAUER, former West Germany captain, correctly predicting England's failure after first match of European Championship finals in Sweden, *1992.*

People said Steve Davis wasn't entertaining. They said the England rugby team wasn't entertaining. What is entertaining? We're not out here to entertain, but to get results.

> CARLTON PALMER, England midfielder, defending the team during finals, *1992.*

Whatever happened to football – passing, that sort of thing?

> BOBBY CHARLTON, former England captain, after match v Denmark, *1992.*

The presence of Manchester City's Paul Lake would have presented them with the all-powerful triumvirate of Merson, Lake and Palmer, which would have been fitting really, given that for most of the tournament England displayed about as much subtlety as a bombastic 70s supergroup.

> THE ABSOLUTE GAME, Scottish fanzine, *1992.*

We know we are probably the best in the world at playing 4–4–2.

> GRAHAM TAYLOR, England manager, abandoning the sweeper system in Sweden but to no avail, *1992.*

Faroe Isles

These are boys who live on barren islands in the middle of the Atlantic and have to fight for their living.

> PAUL GUDLAUGSON, Faroes coach, after a 1–0 European Championship victory over Austria, *1990.*

Germany

We began preparing for penalties as soon as we qualified for the last 16. There was always the chance it could happen.

> FRANZ BECKENBAUER, Germany manager, after his team had beaten England on penalties in the World Cup semi-final, *1990.*

Halifax Town

The idea that football is solely about winning is one of the sicknesses pervading it. Jim McCalliog [manager] is not a general and it isn't a war. But I wouldn't mind a goal.

> DAVE HELLIWELL, Leader of Calderdale Council and Halifax chairman, as the club went nine hours without scoring, *1990*.

The pride factor is as strong at The Shay as it is at Anfield. There are just fewer of us feeling that pride, that's all.

> JIM MCCALLIOG, Halifax manager, *1990*.

Do you know the three most used words in football? Halifax Town Nil.

> JOHN MCGRATH, McCalliog's successor as manager, *1991*.

I'm going to have to listen to offers for all my players – and the club cat, Benny, who is pissed off because there are no mice to catch because they have all died of starvation.

> MCGRATH, on his club's worsening financial plight, *1992*.

Hartlepool United

The listening bank refused to listen and the bank which likes to say yes said no.

> GARRY GIBSON, Hartlepool chairman, on his club's fight against an Inland Revenue winding-up petition, *1993*.

Leeds United

When we open the museum in our new stand it will be full of photographs, medals, cups and everything else connected with the Revie era, and in one corner will be a little memento to what this team has done. Everyone will be happy then, won't they?

> HOWARD WILKINSON, Leeds manager, on comparisons between Don Revie's team and his champions, *1992*.

When my predecessors discovered success it came as a surprise. We had no history. Then it became an accepted part of life. It's only when you lose it that you realise how magical it was. There are kids coming today who cannot have any recollection of Revie. But the magic is passed down from father to son and the hunger becomes insatiable.

> LESLIE SILVER, Leeds chairman, *1990*.

At the start of the season our initial aim was to qualify for Europe. The fact that we are in the European Cup is a bonus, and now we must start thinking like champions.

SILVER, *1992*.

Leeds have won the title because they made fewer mistakes than anybody else all along the way.

ALEX FERGUSON, Manchester United manager, after his team were overhauled by Leeds, *1992*.

There is a stereotype that goes with a lot of clubs. Spurs are called stylish. West Ham is the football academy, Arsenal are resilient. But Leeds are always seen as cynical and intimidating. It becomes a tired cliché.

WILKINSON, *1991*.

We don't take Liverpool's cast-offs.

SILVER, dismissing stories that Leeds were to sign Dean Saunders, *1992*.

I shouldn't have gone. I thought I could go there and win the European Cup. As things turned out, I'm not sure we ever won the toss.

BRIAN CLOUGH, on his 1974 spell with Leeds, *1991*.

Leeds are a big club these days, and a successful one too. I'm also glad to see they've recovered financially since paying me off a few years ago.

CLOUGH, *1991*.

Liverpool

We have a motto at Anfield: If you can't sign the player you want, never sign the second best.

PETER ROBINSON, Liverpool chief executive, *1990*.

They have a lot of good players, it's true, but in Barnes and Rush they have two from a different planet.

RON ATKINSON, Sheffield Wednesday manager, *1990*.

I dread to think what would have happened to my life if I had not come to Liverpool. It was the only place I wanted to go to from Celtic, and 13 years on I'm still grateful they asked me.

KENNY DALGLISH, Liverpool player-manager, announcing his retirement as a player, *1990*.

At Millwall I got the ball every 10 minutes. Here I was getting it every 10 seconds. I don't think I'll keep up with that pace.

JIMMY CARTER, Liverpool winger signed from Millwall, on his debut, *1991*.

Where's the crisis? I don't know. If this is a crisis, you should have been at some of the clubs I've been at.

DAVID SPEEDIE, Liverpool striker, after Dalglish's shock resignation, *1991*.

There is obviously something wrong with the chemistry of the club when so many players are coming and going. It is as if the opportunity to create a good atmosphere has disappeared. When did you last hear of an established player wanting to leave Liverpool? If a player was over the top in the past you didn't hear about it until a new man was in a red shirt.

GLENN HYSEN, Liverpool and Sweden defender, on the new regime of Graeme Souness, *1991*.

Nobody is happy here, but nobody talks about it. No one is thriving at Liverpool. In the corridor, offices and changing room, the climate is bad.

HYSEN, *1991*.

We've got international players here who are not helping the younger ones. When the going gets tough it appears it's the younger players who want to stand up and be counted.

GRAEME SOUNESS, Liverpool manager, on his club's struggles, *1992*.

Envy is the worst fault in human nature. This club has been the most successful in history and people have waited a long time to have a go at Liverpool. Now they've got the chance.

SOUNESS, on Liverpool's decline, *1992*.

I'm joining one of the greatest clubs in the world. But I'll still be young enough to go abroad, and there's a clause in our deal to cover that.

MICHAEL THOMAS, Arsenal midfielder, signing for Liverpool, *1991*.

I thought there might be eight goals but I never thought we would get four of them.

DAVE LANCASTER, Chesterfield striker, after scoring twice in 4–4 League Cup draw at Anfield, *1992*.

Beating them isn't special any more.

BRIAN GAYLE, Sheffield United captain, on his side's 1–0 win over Liverpool, *1992*.

Manchester United

At six o'clock, out of pure curiosity, I turned on my television set. As the news came on, the screen seemed to go black. The normally urbane voice of the announcer seemed to turn into a sledge hammer. My eyes went deathly cold and I sat listening with a frozen brain to that cruel and shocking list of casualties that was now to give the word Munich an even sadder meaning than it had acquired on a day before the war . . .

H. E. BATES, on the 'Busby Babes', *The FA Year Book, 1959.*

In the United States, they call the Dallas Cowboys America's team; Manchester United must then be England's team. They are The Club. The slogan they themselves have adopted in these days of serious marketing proclaims them The World's Greatest Football Club. No one has yet complained to the Advertising Standards Authority.

IAN RIDLEY, author, *Season in the Cold: A Journey Through English Football, 1992.*

I had to get rid of this idea that Manchester United were a drinking club, rather than a football club.

ALEX FERGUSON, United manager, on his problems with Norman Whiteside and Paul McGrath, in *Six Years at United, 1992.*

ICI is a world-class business. There is no way it would want to buy a second-class football team.

CITY ANALYST, quoted in *Sunday Times* on rumours that ICI were interested in buying United, *1990.*

If you don't accept the pressure and the fact that you're going to be in the limelight, you'll go under.

NEIL WEBB, England midfielder, on playing for United, *1990.*

There's Only One United

GEOFFREY GREEN book title, *1978.*

There's only one United – the biscuit

BADGE slogan seen at Anfield, *1990.*

This team makes you suffer. I deserve a million pounds a year to have this job.

FERGUSON, **after drawn FA Cup Final with Crystal Palace,** *1990.*

Montrose

I thought I'd come to a chicken factory. It was also reminiscent of a Chinese women's volleyball team.

IVO DEN BIEMEN, Dutch striker, giving his first (surreal) impressions of the Scottish club, *1990.*

Nottingham Forest

We do so little pre-season training we're only just getting fit.

> STUART PEARCE, Forest captain, after his side's poor start to the season, *1992*.

The only person certain of boarding the coach for the Littlewoods Cup Final is Albert Kershaw, and he'll be driving it.

> BRIAN CLOUGH, Forest manager, keeping his players on their toes before the League Cup Final, *1990*.

The team has no bottle. If the going gets tough you need more than just ball players, you need a Vinnie Jones. He'd liven the place up.

> HANS SEGERS, Wimbledon and former Forest goalkeeper, as his old club slid towards relegation, *1993*.

Notts County

I thought at one stage about playing a sweeper and trying to get a draw, but then I thought 'what the hell'. Our natural game is suicidal football with everyone charging forward, and it wouldn't be fair to ask the lads to change.

> NEIL WARNOCK, County manager, before the team's FA Cup tie at Tottenham, *1991*.

Oldham Athletic

We couldn't buy the amount of publicity the football club has given us. Companies that didn't even know the place existed have suddenly heard of us.

> JOHN BATTYE, Oldham Council Leader, on the rewards for the club's Cup runs, *1990*.

Oldham Athletic? That's a contradiction in terms.

> *CORONATION STREET* character, *1980s*.

Port Vale

The reason she [Samantha Fox] is so big in Eastern Europe and the Third World is that they're neglected in terms of the range of talent prepared to visit them, so even a small star becomes big once they arrive. In football terms, she's been playing Port Vale instead of Arsenal.

> MAX CLIFFORD, showbiz agent, *1991*.

Queen of the South

The Queen of the South shall rise up in the judgment with the men of this generation and condemn them.

> LUKE 11:31, New Testament. The Dumfries club are the only football team mentioned in The Bible.

Rangers

It was like trying to carry a ton weight up the down escalator. You wonder how Scotland could ever lose a football match.

> HOWARD WILKINSON, Leeds manager, after his team's European Cup defeat by the Scottish champions, *1992*.

Rangers may be a big club commercially but in football terms Liverpool are still the No. 1 in Britain.

> GRAEME SOUNESS on leaving the Rangers managership for Liverpool, *1991*.

I'm often asked how this Rangers team compares with Celtic's Lisbon Lions of '67. I have to be honest and say I think it'd be a draw, but then some us are getting on for 60.

> BERTIE AULD, former Celtic midfielder, as Rangers, narrowly failed to reach the European Cup Final, *1993*.

Republic of Ireland

The Irish force an unattractive game on the opposition. No team has managed to escape this contagious crap.

> AHMED EL-MOKADEM, Egypt official, after 0–0 draw v Ireland, World Cup finals, *1990*.

Before the game Tony Cascarino said, 'You'll never believe the way we play.' I said it can't be that bad, but it was worse.

> GORDON COWANS, Cascarino's Aston Villa colleague, after encountering Ireland's 'direct' approach, *1990*.

One day someone might pat us on the head and tell us we've got the game right.

> JACK CHARLTON, Ireland manager, *1991*.

Charlton may have been looking at Motherwell's Nick Cusack, who has an Irish grandparent or perhaps owns an Irish setter.

> JAMES TRAYNOR, football correspondent, *Glasgow Herald, 1990*.

Of course, we play a lot more football at United.

> DENNIS IRWIN, Manchester United and Republic of Ireland full-back on differences between his club international football, *1990*.

Look at the Irish. They sing and none of them know the words. Jack sings, and all he knows is 'Blaydon Races' and 'Cushy Butterfield'. But look at the pride they have in those green shirts.

> LAWRIE MCMENEMY, England assistant manager, calling for Graham Taylor's players to sing the national anthem, *1991*.

They are the poor man's Republic of Ireland.

> GRAHAM TAYLOR, England manager, on the unsuitability of the tour of Australia and New Zealand as a testing ground for international players, *1991*.

Scotland

A good team with strong English character.

> RUUD GULLIT, Netherlands striker, before match v Scotland, *1992*.

We've been playing for an hour and it's just occurred to me that we're drawing 0–0 with a mountain top.

> IAN ARCHER, Radio Scotland pundit, during San Marino v Scotland match, *1991*. The Scots eventually won 2–0.

Sheffield United

Sheffield Eagles [rugby league team] play the ball on the ground more than Sheffield United do.

> JONATHAN FOSTER, journalist, *The Independent, 1990*.

We've been tested over the last few weeks and a lot of the players have failed. They don't realise it because they're too thick.

> DAVE BASSETT, United manager, after 5–2 defeat at Arsenal, *1991*.

Lucan Alive! Found in Sheffield United Trophy Room.

> COVER SLOGAN, *War of the Monster Trucks,* Sheffield Wednesday fanzine, *1993*.

Sheffield Wednesday

The criterion I have always used to judge my teams is: 'Do I enjoy watching them?' Right now I enjoy watching Wednesday very much.

> RON ATKINSON, Wednesday manager, *1990*.

The big-city team with the small-town mentality. I once compared them with Ipswich and drew howls of disapproval from some quarters. But at the time, the analogy was true.

> HOWARD WILKINSON, Leeds and former Wednesday manager, *1991*.

It's like having a prison sentence quashed.

> ATKINSON, on Wednesday's return to the First Division, *1991*.

Southampton

If he can let teams come here and play like that, and if that is the standard of refereeing, then English football has no future.

> GRAEME SOUNESS, Liverpool manager, after a bruising draw with Southampton, *1992*.

We don't have a dirty player on the books.

> IAN BRANFOOT, Southampton manager, replying to Souness. The 'Saints' had the worst disciplinary record in the First Division in 1991–92.

Players responsible for 33 per cent of our offences have left the club, so that should help.

> BRANFOOT, after Southampton were fined £20,000 for their disciplinary record, with £15,000 suspended against good behaviour, *1992*.

Swindon Town

I don't think there's a better footballing side in the Second Division than us, but perhaps good footballing sides don't always get their just rewards.

> GLENN HODDLE, Swindon player-manager, *1992*.

Tottenham Hotspur

Betrayal is a strong word, but I can't think of a better one to describe what has been done behind my back. I have always said what I wanted most was to stay with Paul Gascoigne and Terry Venables at Spurs. But now I know that they want to sell me it puts a very different complexion on how I feel about them.

GARY LINEKER, after learning that hard-up Spurs were trying to sell him to an Italian club, *1991*.

Wales

Players like Barry Horne and Peter Nicholas have always knocked opponents down, but now they have learned the old Norman Hunter trick of shaking hands and helping them up. In the old days, we'd knock them down and then want to fight them. In fairness I was probably the leader of the pack.

TERRY YORATH, Wales manager, *1991*.

West Ham United

I don't know if we can help the Hammers or not, but we're going to pray for them.

BILLY GRAHAM, evangelist, addressing a rally at Upton Park, *1989*.

That 'happy losers' stuff is a lot of cobblers. We're not good losers here. I hate losing.

BILLY BONDS, West Ham manager, *1991*.

The West Ham performance was obscene in the sense of the effort they put into the match.

ALEX FERGUSON, Manchester United manager, on West Ham's 1–0 defeat of his championship-chasing side, in *Six Years at United, 1992*.

Wimbledon

We have to remain the English bulldog SAS club. We have to sustain ourselves by sheer power and the attitude that we will kick ass. We are an academy. We find gems and turn them into finished articles.

SAM HAMMAM, Wimbledon chairman, *1992*.

Before we go down, we'll leave a stream of blood from here to Timbuktoo.

HAMMAM, *1992*.

This team is nothing like the one I had at Wimbledon. That team would have been all right against Frazier and Tyson.

DAVE BASSETT, Sheffield United manager, *1992*.

They tell me even Wimbledon are playing good football.

BOBBY ROBSON, PSV Eindhoven manager, *1992*.

We haven't changed our style. It's comical and we've all had a good laugh about it in the dressing room.

ALAN CORK, Wimbledon striker, on reports that the Dons were playing a passing game, *1990*.

They can wear jeans and earrings for all I care, but I draw the line at stockings and suspenders – until after the match.

JOE KINNEAR, Wimbledon manager, on predecessor Peter Withe's no-jeans rule, *1992*.

Playing in front of 4000 at Wimbledon becomes depressing after a time.

TERRY PHELAN, on his move to Manchester City, *1992*.

They got 6000? I can't for the life of me see how they get that many each week. The fans would be better off going shopping.

HOWARD KENDALL, Manchester City manager, after draw at Plough Lane, *1990*.

Personally I take special pride in our low gates and the fact that we continue to fight against the odds. This we will continue to do as long as we are supported by one person.

HAMMAM, *1992*.

Everyone was drunk the night before, every single one of us was down the pub. Probably what won us the FA Cup Final. That, and taking me off after 60 minutes because I was delirious.

CORK, on their 1988 Wembley win, *1991*.

Wolverhampton Wanderers

I had a book of excuses for people who rang up and said: 'Where's my money?' We couldn't even pay the milk bill.

KEITH PEARSON, Wolves secretary, looking back at the club's 1980s brushes with extinction, *1993*.

CHAPTER 2

Managing to Survive

If you're a manager you don't have fitted carpets.

JOHN BARNWELL shortly before his sacking by Walsall, *1990*.

Fulham Football Club seek a Manager/Genius.

NEWSPAPER advert, *1991*.

Football management these days is like a nuclear war. No winners, just survivors.

TOMMY DOCHERTY, manager of more than a dozen clubs, *1992*.

As a manager you're like a prostitute. You depend on other people for your living.

STEVE COPPELL, Crystal Palace manager, reflecting on how a dubious refereeing decision led to his side's FA Cup defeat at Hartlepool, *1993*.

From Monday to Friday a manager's job is superb. It's the other bit that can be a problem.

ALEX MACDONALD on his dismissal by Hearts, *1991*.

It's a great job apart from Saturday afternoons. Happy? Football managers are never happy. You've always got to be moaning at someone.

JOCKY SCOTT, Dunfermline manager, after his team's first win in 19 matches, *1991*.

You sit on the touchline and moan at them for not having it. Then you realise that if they did they'd not be playing non-League football.

RAY WILKIE, Barrow manager, *1991*.

I love football but I positively hate being a manager.

LOU MACARI, West Ham manager, *1989*.

When I told Graham [Taylor] about the job he sent my wife a bouquet of flowers and told me my troubles were just beginning.

> JOHN WARD, former assistant to Taylor at Aston Villa, on becoming York City manager, *1991*.

It's not as bad as it sounds. We played some good stuff in patches. A lot of good things did come out of the game.

> JOE BOON, Worthing manager, after his team's 13–0 defeat by Carshalton in the Vauxhall League, *1991*.

I have learned more about football in the past six months than in 25 years as a player.

> BILLY BONDS, West Ham manager, *1990*.

When I was appointed manager of Stoke the first phone call I received was from Joe Mercer, then with Aston Villa, offering his congratulations. He told me, 'My advice is never to trust anyone in the game,and when I put down this phone don't trust me either.'

> TONY WADDINGTON, former Stoke manager,*1990*.

I've heard it said that you can't be a football manager and tell the truth. Well, I'm going to have a go at it.

> LIAM BRADY on becoming Celtic manager,*1991*.

There isn't another industry in the world like soccer where the players still call the manager 'Boss' or 'Gaffer'. It's a joke, isn't it? A sort of throwback to the days of Victorian mill-owners.

> JON HOLMES, agent, in Colin Malam, *Gary Lineker: Strikingly Different*, *1992*.

You hope and you pretend you know what you're doing.

> KEVIN KEEGAN on the art of management, shortly after joining Newcastle,*1992*.

We made him an offer he should have refused.

> MIKE BATESON, Torquay chairman, on appointing Ivan Golac as manager, *1992*.

The pressure on match days is making my head explode. I can't go on.

> KENNY DALGLISH proferring his resignation to the Liverpool board, *1991*.

If Kenny Dalglish has resigned because of the pressures of the job, the rest of us have no chance. He had the players and financial resources.

> HOWARD WILKINSON, Leeds manager, *1991*.

'The only English I've heard from him is goal.' Manchester United's Steve Bruce on Eric Cantona, pictured above left using his French to claim a foul

'I've pushed this club to the top – I've been the face of AC Milan.' Ruud Gullit (ABOVE RIGHT) modestly assesses his impact in Italy

'Referees should be policemen on traffic duty, not conductors in an orchestra.' Gordon Taylor, PFA. BELOW: Sweden's Bo Karlsson takes the point

'Old Trafford is buzzing with atmosphere even when it's empty . . . it's like a cathedral.' Tommy Docherty, ex-United manager and regular worshipper

'In Glasgow, half the fans hate you and the other half think they own you.' Tommy Burns, former Celtic player. BELOW: the great divide

'The police have got my passport, but football takes all my pressures away.'
ABOVE: Mickey Thomas organising Wrexham's wall while facing currency charges

'I never thought any player was worth £3.3 million until I saw Alan Shearer play for Blackburn.' Alan Hansen on Shearer (BELOW)

'I'd rather die and have vultures eat my insides than merge with Crystal Palace.' Sam Hammam (ABOVE LEFT), Wimbledon's Lebanese chairman

'In many ways he's an absolute ignorant pig, but he does care about the club.' Barry Fry, then Barnet manager, on Stan Flashman (ABOVE RIGHT)

'He portrays a happy-go-lucky image, but he doesn't fool the players.' Kevin Moran on Ron Atkinson (BELOW)

Pressure? What pressure?

GEORGE GRAHAM, Arsenal manager, the weekend after Dalglish's resignation, *1991*.

Five grand a week? That's my kind of pressure.

LOU MACARI, Birmingham manager, after former Celtic team-mate Dalglish's shock departure, *1991*.

When you're a manager it's the same whether you're spending £3 million or £30,000 – pressure goes with the job.

PHIL NEAL, Bolton manager and former Liverpool captain, *1991*.

We all know it's a precarious job. Monday to Friday is quite easy. It's Saturdays that are the problem. Kenny's pressure was to keep on succeeding. Mine is to succeed at all.

CHRIS MCMENEMY, Chesterfield manager, *1991*.

My eldest son is playing in goal for Halifax reserves – and I think I've got pressure!

BOBBY GOULD on taking over as West Brom manager, *1991*.

Pressure to me is being homeless or unemployed. This isn't pressure, it's pleasure.

ANDY ROXBURGH, Scotland coach, after losing 17 'first picks' to injury from squad to face Germany, *1993*.

Pressure? You are under pressure in war zones, not in football.

ARTHUR COX, Derby manager, *1993*.

Everyone has pressure, whatever walk of life they are in. I happen to like the aggravation that goes with football management – it seems to suit my needs.

GRAEME SOUNESS, on day he was appointed Liverpool manager in succession to Dalglish, *1991*.

It's like being in the middle of an oven.

BOB PEARSON, Millwall manager and former chief scout, on his new job after latest in a lengthy run of defeats, *1990*.

It was like being in the dentist's chair for six hours.

HOWARD WILKINSON, Leeds United manager, after tense Leeds v Leicester match, *1990*.

It's not too good for the old grey hairs.

GERRY FRANCIS, QPR manager, *1991*.

I hate watching. It's making me go grey.

> PETER REID, Manchester City player-manager, *1991*.

I'm past the Kenny Dalglish stage. I've gone potty. I've been there and I'm coming back.

> TERRY VENABLES, Tottenham chief executive, on his attempts to buy control of the club, *1991*.

When you win you feel 25, when you lose you feel more like 105.

> GORDON LEE, Leicester manager, after 5–2 defeat at Swindon, *1991*.

Sometimes I wish I was a gardener.

> KENNY HIBBITT, Walsall manager, on the strain of watching his team defend a lead at Lincoln, *1992*.

Who'd be a football manager? It's not good for your heart.

> ANDY ROXBURGH, Scotland coach, after 2–2 draw v Switzerland, *1991*.

I think my team are trying to kill me.

> JOE ROYLE, Oldham manager, after nerve-wracking but successful fight against relegation, *1993*.

Watching that goal go in I felt like Monica Seles. It was like somebody sticking a big knife in my back.

> JOHN BOND, Shrewsbury manager, after defeat by Northampton cost his team a place in the Third Division play-offs, *1993*.

I was manager of Purfleet in the Vauxhall League and wound myself up about a game at Woking. On the coach back, I just fainted. I couldn't move or understand anything that was going on. Even now I can't quite speak properly and have to see the doctor six times a week. It was all down to blood pressure.

> HARRY CRIPPS, former Millwall full-back, after suffering a heart attack, *1990*.

I had to choose between tobacco and football and I chose football.

> JOHAN CRUYFF, Barcelona manager and 40-a day smoker until his heart bypass operation, *1992*.

Not only have I had to give up chess because I don't have the time any more, but I'm also smoking myself to death. If we go through and win the play-offs at Wembley, I'll be smoking more than my old boss [Cesar] Menotti.

> OSSIE ARDILES, Swindon manager, *1990*.

About 10 years ago, I learned how to relieve managerial stress. When the ball gets into your last third, avert your eyes. Turn to your physio, ask for chewing gum, have a few words about the match, anything. It stops the tension building up. You might miss a goal, but why worry? Someone can always tell you how it happened.

BILLY BINGHAM, Northern Ireland manager, *1992*.

There is no crisis here. Just panic.

JOHN DOCHERTY, Millwall manager, *after seven successive defeats, 1989*.

I'm sweating more on the bench than some of my players on the field.

JOHN TOSHACK, Real Madrid coach, *1989*.

If I wasn't the manager I'd have gone home early.

ALEX MILLER, Hibernian manager, *after 0–0 draw, 1992*.

I felt like booing myself.

DAVE MACKAY, Birmingham manager, *after drab goalless draw v Wigan, 1990*.

I feel twice as bad as any adjective you want to use.

BILLY AYRE, Halifax manager, *after home defeat, 1989*.

Don't ask me if it was a good game. It would be like asking a surgeon if it was a good operation.

HOWARD WILKINSON, Leeds manager, *after rugged match at West Ham, 1989*.

We really go through it on the bench. Last night when we were 2–1 up and they got a couple of late corners the others were all laughing at me because I was curled up in a ball in the corner of the dug-out saying, 'I hate this job.'

BRIAN LITTLE, Leicester manager, *1993*.

I don't want to say anything I might regret.

MEL MACHIN, Barnsley manager, *in message to waiting reporters explaining he would not be attending the customary post-match press conference, after 4–1 defeat at Newcastle, 1990*.

Playing was great. Managing was unrewarding and stupid.

GEOFF HURST, former England World Cup player and ex-Chelsea manager, *1991*.

I left as I arrived – fired with enthusiasm.

JOHN MCGRATH, Halifax manager, *on getting sacked by Preston, 1991*.

67

I'd advise anyone to play as long as possible, even if it's only in the park on a Sunday afternoon. That is the best game. Managing is a poor second.

GRAEME SOUNESS, Liverpool manager, *1992*.

Things got so bad I received a letter from *Reader's Digest* saying I hadn't been included in their prize draw.

> JOHN MCGRATH, on life after being sacked by Halifax, *1993*.

How ironic that this should happen on the anniversary of the Coventry blitz. When I received the phone call from the chairman it felt like my house had just been bombed.

> JOHN SILLETT on his dismissal as Coventry manager, *1990*.

It was like opening a book I've read before. I knew the lines.

> NORMAN HUNTER, former England defender, on being sacked as Bradford City coach, *1990*.

There's no animosity in my heart today, but I'll be distraught tomorrow because I won't have a football problem to deal with.

> DAVID PLEAT, on being sacked by Leicester, *1991*.

There have been been better managers than me sacked, but now I am just a statistic – the 543rd manager to be sacked since the war.

> PLEAT, as above.

I told the chairman, Mr Bateson, to back me or sack me. He sacked me.

> JOHN IMPEY, former Torquay manager, dismissed four months after leading the club to promotion, *1991*.

When Leeds sacked me all my worries about pensions and bringing up three kids were gone, and I became a better manager.

> BRIAN CLOUGH on his £90,000 'golden handshake' from Leeds 16 years earlier, *1990*.

It's not the sort of job I crave. You don't often get the appreciation you deserve.

> GARY LINEKER on management after Spurs sacked Peter Shreeves, *1992*.

Why should I be sacked when it's the players who go out and make the mistakes?

> VUJADIN BOSKOV, Sampdoria coach, *1991*.

Sacking a manager is as big an event in my life as drinking a glass of beer. I'd hire 20 managers a year if I wanted to – 100 if necessary.

> JESUS GIL, president of Atletico Madrid, after dismissing Ron Atkinson, *1989*.

I see Atletico [Madrid] just sacked another manager before the season has even started. He must have had a bad photocall.

RON ATKINSON, *1990*.

Even when he is making love he is thinking of Atletico Madrid.

JESUS GIL, on one of Atkinson's short-lived successors, Tomislav Ivic, *1991*.

It could be worse. I could be the Manageress and she's pregnant.

JIM SMITH, Newcastle manager, resigning on health grounds, *1991*. *The Manageress* was a TV drama series about a female football manager.

I'm not coming here to be miserable. I've come here to enjoy every day and to make sure everyone around me smiles.

BOBBY GOULD, West Brom manager, *1991*.

If I see anyone without a smile on his face, he'll be sacked.

BRIAN FLYNN, Wrexham manager, on being bottom of the Football League, *1990*.

I've never felt under less pressure in my life. All that is on my mind is whether I'll catch a fish tomorrow.

JOHN LYALL, Ipswich manager, during promotion run-in, *1992*.

This is my life, I haven't got anything else. I break the speed limit every morning driving to the training ground. I love every minute of it and every problem it presents.

ARTHUR COX, Derby manager, *1993*.

I'm happy. We've got a point and I've not lost my money in a pension fund.

GRAEME SOUNESS, Liverpool manager, after his team's draw at Southampton soon after the Maxwell/MGN scandal, *1992*.

It's the best day since I got married.

ALEX FERGUSON, Manchester United manager, after winning at Sheffield United, *1992*.

When I stopped playing and was out of the game, I was cutting grass and washing cars – this is better.

JIM RYAN, Luton manager, *1990*.

How can anybody call this work? People in this game don't realise how lucky they are. You drive to the ground, play a few five-a-sides, then have lunch. It's wonderful, enjoyable fun.

RON ATKINSON, Aston Villa manager, *1993*

If the League rang tomorrow and asked to paint the grass pink, I'd be out there with my toothbrush.

> BARRY FRY, Barnet manager, on eve of club's first season in Football League, *1991*.

I always say I'll get over it when I grow up, but there are no signs of it happening yet. I still find it impossible to drive past any sort of match. I've got to stop and watch it.

> CRAIG BROWN, Scotland assistant manager, *1988*.

I'll go anywhere to watch a match, as the wife will tell you. I stopped in the other night because there were no games, and it was the first time I'd noticed that we'd got a colour TV.

> CHRIS WRIGHT, Sutton Coldfield Town manager, *1992*.

When you have friends in the game you want them to do well – but not as well as you.

> COLIN HARVEY, Everton manager, on his predecessor (and successor) Howard Kendall, *1990*.

I socialise, I still enjoy a laugh and a beer with the players, but you have to know when to go. You need to be a little detached. There are tough decisions to be made at times, and they'd be even tougher if you were too close.

> PETER REID of Manchester City, on the player-manager's life, *1991*.

Winning European Cups gave me a half-decent start in management, but the instant respect you get from players only lasts three minutes.

> MARTIN O'NEILL, Wycombe Wanderers manager and ex-Nottingham Forest midfielder, *1993*.

Q: Best mates at club?
A: Managers have very few.

> JOHN RUDGE, Port Vale manager, answering programme questionnaire, *1993*.

One thing I have learned about management is that you don't fall in love with players.

> GRAHAM TAYLOR, England manager, *1992*.

When I was at Celtic I was said to be a players' man and maybe that was true. In those days if the ship was sinking I would have thrown all 11 lifebelts to the players. Now I would keep one for myself, throw 10 and lose a player.

> DAVID HAY, St Mirren manager, on the lessons of his dismissal by Celtic, *1991*.

It's certainly embarrassing for me. That's why I stayed in the bath for half an hour afterwards. I thought you lot would have buggered off by now.

> BARRY FRY, Barnet manager, to reporters after a 5–0 home defeat by Portsmouth, FA Cup, *1991*.

We welcome the Directors and Staff of Chester City, especially manager Harry McNally, who has recently been in hospital. I hope today's game does not help to improve his health.

> SAM ELLIS, Bury manager, programme column, *1990*.

It's hard to be passionate twice a week.

> GEORGE GRAHAM, Arsenal manager, on the draining effects of a crowded schedule, *1991*.

I've told the players we need to win so that I can have the cash to buy some new ones.

> CHRIS TURNER, Peterborough manager, before League Cup quarter-final v Middlesbrough, *1992*.

If it meant getting three points on Saturday I'd shoot my grandmother. Not nastily, I would just hurt her.

> BRIAN CLOUGH, Nottingham Forest manager, on life at foot of the Premier League, *1992*.

That's not the worst reception I've ever had – did you ever see me as a player?

> BOBBY GOULD, West Brom manager, after demonstration against him by fans, *1992*.

Everybody called me to tell me what to do. I heard from the President, two former presidents and the Opposition leader.

> CARLOS BILARDO, Argentina coach, after defeat in World Cup Final, *1990*.

Journalist: Villa's transfer turnover has been £11 million in five weeks since [Ron] Atkinson arrived.
Bobby Gould: I'll be happy if I get 11p to spend this week.

> EXCHANGE at West Brom manager's press briefing, *1991*.

If I had £1.5 million to spend, I would have to buy a grandstand.

> NEIL WARNOCK, Notts County manager, as the Taylor Report began to take effect, *1991*.

We'll probably buy a few more at £40,000, though the chairman might let me go to 60 grand for Ian Rush.

> DAVE BASSETT, Sheffield United manager, on his club's shoestring success, *1990*.

I saw our bank manager this morning and he was smiling. He even gave me a cup of coffee.

> BARRY LLOYD, Brighton manager, after his debt-ridden club drew Manchester United in the Coca-Cola Cup, *1992*.

To be honest I thought in extra time both teams had settled for a replay. I was panicking then, because I hadn't re-booked our hotel for midweek.

> STEVE COPPELL, Crystal Palace manager, on his side's FA Cup semi-final victory over Liverpool, *1990*.

All coaches want to prove something, but the amount of self-justification that goes on these days makes you want to puke. You continually come across it in match reports that are almost entirely devoted to how results were achieved. Not by the players, but the managers. It's as though some of them are saying: 'This doesn't happen very often so I'd better take the opportunity of proving to everybody how good I am.'

> HOWARD WILKINSON, Leeds manager, *1992*.

One of the coaches at Brighton, Brian Eastick, made us play five-a-side without the ball. I scored the best hat-trick ever seen.

> ANDY RITCHIE, Oldham and former Brighton striker, *1993*.

There are two types of people who succeed in coaching: the conman and confidence trickster or the intelligent man who builds your confidence and belief. I'm the conman.

> MALCOLM ALLISON, on becoming Bristol Rovers' chief coach aged 65, *1992*.

I found it difficult scoring goals for Partick Thistle. That's something I always keep in mind when telling Mo Johnston how it's done. That's part of the irony of coaching. You have to keep your ego in check. I'm not Frank Sinatra, I'm the stage manager.

> ANDY ROXBURGH, Scotland coach, *1990*.

When Mick Channon was asked what made a good manager he would always answer 'good players' and a lot of the time I agreed with him. Now I would say that good managers can make very good players.

> MARTIN O'NEILL, Wycombe Wanderers manager and former Northern Ireland captain, *1992*.

I admit that I'm to blame for our performances this season, just as I was to blame for the 108 goals we scored last season.

> JOHN TOSHACK, on being sacked by Real Madrid, *1990*.

I told him that even though they're building the Channel Tunnel it just wouldn't be possible for me to drive back from Marseille every night.

> RON ATKINSON revealing he had turned down an approach from Marseille shortly after leaving Sheffield Wednesday because of the travelling, *1991*.

It's a tough draw. Last season Benfica played 38 games like us and lost only one, the same as us. They conceded only 18 goals, the same as us, but they scored more than we did, 89 to our 74. I don't know a lot about them.

> GEORGE GRAHAM, Arsenal manager, *1991*.

A win today is essential – anything less would put us too far adrift of the teams above us.

> ALAN BALL, Stoke manager, programme column, *1989*.

Never believe everything you read in programmes – some managers don't even write their own articles.

> BALL to reporter who asked him about the consequences of defeat after the game.

I'm definitely maybe going to play Sturrock.

> JIM MCLEAN, Dundee United manager, *1986*.

The manager's indecision is final.

> LEEDS players' catchphrase about one of Don Revie's successors, *1970s*.

What would I watch them for? I find it amazing that they should come and watch us. If I was a professional manager and my team couldn't beat Barrow . . . .

> RAY WILKIE, Barrow manager, before his non-League part-timers' FA Cup tie with Bolton, *1991*.

I never thought I'd see the day when I'd say we needed more Englishmen in our squad.

> ALEX FERGUSON, Glaswegian manager of Manchester United, on UEFA's restrictions on 'foreigners', *1991*.

We went to Liverpool, attacked them, thought we were the better team, and were 3–0 down at half-time. You stand in the dressing room and think: This isn't fair.

> FERGUSON, after 4–0 defeat at Anfield, *1990*.

Something will happen somewhere in the 89th minute that will either break somebody's heart or make their day.

> BRIAN LITTLE, Leicester manager, as the promotion and relegation battles went into the season's last day, *1992*.

Listening to what 700 people at Shawfield [Clyde's former ground] could say when things were going badly inoculated me. Seventy thousand couldn't upset me now.

> CRAIG BROWN, Scotland assistant manager, *1989*.

I've been in football 30 years, and swearing seems part and parcel of the game.

> ALEX TOTTEN, St Johnstone manager, answering breach of the peace charge, Perth sheriff's court, *1992*.

There's not a prayer I want the England job. Anybody who applies for it has to be bloody crackers after the way this business has been handled.

> JACK CHARLTON, Republic of Ireland manager, on the press treatment of Bobby Robson before the World Cup, *1990*.

Blokes like George Graham and Graeme Souness, they have their problems too. It's just that their problems are different – a lot bloody different.

> THEO FOLEY, manager of poverty-stricken Northampton, *1991*.

It's becoming difficult these days to bring good players into your club because of the number of clubs around who seem to need to have nearly two football teams.

> HOWARD WILKINSON, Leeds manager, as the champions struggled, *1992*.

Everybody wants to take on the best and I do too. I want to pit my wits against all of them – Manchester United, Real Madrid, Juventus and Fray Bentos.

> BARRY FRY, newly appointed Southend manager, on his ambitions to manage a big club, *1993*.

It's not like the brochures.

> KEVIN KEEGAN, Newcastle manager, discovering the realities of management, *1992*.

How can I tell my youngsters that this is the best club in the world when the bath is not clean and the toilets are dirty?

> KEEGAN, after spending his first day in charge of Newcastle cleaning up the training ground, *1992*.

I never seem to miss England quite enough. I might only be operating at about 30 per cent of my potential as a manager, but the lifestyle makes up for the rest.

> RODNEY MARSH, Tampa Bay Rowdies chief executive and ex-England player, *1991*.

Sometimes you have to accept there's nothing you can do – extra training, psychology, getting a couple of strippers in, none of it will help.

> DAVE BASSETT, Sheffield United manager, as his team set a club record for games without a win, *1990*.

When you're building a team, you're looking for good players, not blokes to marry your daughters.

> BASSETT, after buying Vinnie Jones, *1990*.

My youngest daughter gets married on Saturday, which is more important than either job.

> GRAHAM TAYLOR, Aston Villa manager, before being confirmed as England manager, *1990*.

We've had letters from accountants, plumbers, electricians and an Army chap who said he knew about discipline and wouldn't hesitate to flog the players at half-time.

> JOHN EVANS, West Brom secretary, on his club's vacant manager's post, *1991*.

When the television people asked me if I'd like to play a football manager in a play, I asked how long it would take. They told me 'about 10 days' and I said: 'That's about par for the course.'

> TOMMY DOCHERTY, former manager, *1989*.

I don't sit down on New Year's Eve and get all emotional and wonder if it's going to be a good year for me. I know it's going to be the year I make it.

> HOWARD WILKINSON, Leeds manager, *1990*.

Something happened to football in the mid-Seventies. Suddenly managers became more important than players. Every magazine you picked up had Brian Clough, Ron Atkinson or Tommy Docherty inside. I don't believe in the cult of management and I don't want to add to it.

> ANDY ROXBURGH, Scotland coach, on why he refuses to do 'personal' interviews, *1990*.

The nice aspect about football captaincy is that, if things go wrong, it's the manager who gets the blame.

> GARY LINEKER, former Leicestershire schools cricket skipper, on being made England captain, *1990*.

You wait a lifetime for a feeling like tonight.

> ALEX FERGUSON, Manchester United manager, after his team celebrated the club's first championship in 26 years, *1993*.

We all end up yesterday's men in this business. You're very quickly forgotten.

> JOCK STEIN, former Celtic manager, in Archie Macpherson, *The Great Derbies: Blue and Green*, *1989*.

CHAPTER 3

The Gaffer

Malcolm Allison

I feel like Red Adair – people only call me when the fire's out of control.

> ALLISON, on becoming 'acting chief coach' at 65 to relegation-threatened Bristol Rovers, *1992*.

Most of the Villa lads are under 25 and won't know who Malcolm is.

> RON ATKINSON, Aston Villa manager, responding to Allison's jibes before FA Cup tie against Rovers, *1993*.

Ossie Ardiles

I learnt a little from each of my managers – from [Cesar] Menotti to smoke, from [Keith] Burkinshaw to play golf.

> ARDILES, Swindon manager, *1990*.

I will never compromise my ideals whatever division I'm in. I tell the boys to try and play like Pele.

> ARDILES as his West Brom team chased promotion from the Second (neé Third) Division, *1993*.

Ron Atkinson

Q: Are you a better manager for your recent experiences?
A: No, I always thought I was good.

> EXCHANGE between journalist and Atkinson, then Sheffield Wednesday manager, *1990*.

I just bumped into Cyrille Regis [a born-again Christian] and I said: 'What's all this crap about you finding God? You worked with him at West Brom for four years.'

> ATKINSON, after Wednesday's League Cup tie at Coventry, *1990*.

He has never slagged off United or criticised anyone here since he left. And he could have made a few bob doing so.

> ALEX FERGUSON, Manchester United manager, before the League Cup Final against Atkinson's Wednesday, *1991*.

Ron has high ideals. He loves his football, and has to like what he sees when his team are playing. If he likes it, he knows the public will too.

> DAVE SEXTON, Aston Villa coach, on his club's manager, *1992*.

It would be easy to be fooled by the happy-go-lucky image he portrays. But believe me, when he hands out a rollicking you know about it. He has developed the art of camouflaging his real feelings, but he doesn't fool the players.

> KEVIN MORAN, Blackburn and former Manchester United defender, *1993*.

Alan Ball

I could manage Tottenham – no danger – and it rankles me that I'm not holding down one of the bigger jobs. People look at me and see this horrible, aggressive little bastard and a racing freak. Nothing could be further from the truth.

> BALL, Exeter manager, *1991*.

Dave 'Harry' Bassett

I know what they are all thinking – the Elephant Man is back, stand well clear. I was once called the spiv in the £400 suit. I felt right insulted. It cost at least a grand.

> BASSETT, Sheffield United manager, on his return to the First Division, *1990*.

John Beck

[Beck] had gone barmy before the game. The [Bristol] City manager, Denis Smith, had said something on the radio, a really over-the-top comment . . . so he said 'Welsh bastards!, meaning Bristol City.

> COLIN BAILLIE, former Cambridge player, on the club's then-manager, *1992*.

Danny Bergara

I sweated and sweated to get there [Wembley], more than any man should have to. I've been given the elbow so many times since starting my first job coaching the amateurs Sheffield FC. Since then I've run myself into the ground, trying to prove that even if you speak funny you can have talent.

> BERGARA, Stockport's Uruguayan manager, *1992*.

Billy Bonds

I'm very surprised he's making such a success of it. As a player, Bonzo would give everything – as long as he was playing. But he was never really that interested in watching football. I don't think he ever went to a reserve game. After training he was always the first off home. But management is all day, every day, so I did wonder if it would suit him.

> HARRY REDKNAPP, Bournemouth manager, on his former West Ham team-mate, a year before becoming his assistant, *1991*.

Sir Matt Busby

He has held his magnetism right through five decades. I remember in Rotterdam for the final of the Cup Winners' Cup a lot of fans were gathered at the main entrance chanting the names of players like 'Hughesy' as they went in. Suddenly Sir Matt arrived and the wild cheering turned into respectful applause. It was quite touching, just like the Pope arriving.

> ALEX FERGUSON, Manchester United manager, in *Six Years at United, 1992*.

His greatest achievement was to create the illusion of beauty in a craft wretchedly deformed from the beginning.

> EAMON DUNPHY, United reserve during Busby era, in *A Strange Kind of Glory, 1991*.

Jack Charlton

Jack is not always right, but he is never wrong.

> JOHNY GILES, former Republic of Ireland manager and ex-Leeds team-mate, *1991*.

Jack cracks me up. He makes out he's not really interested in football, and tells the whole world he's going fishing. But we know what he's thinking about when he's fishing. Football.

> JOHAN CRUYFF, Barcelona manager, *1990*.

He could argue anything with anyone.

> PAT CHARLTON, his wife, *1990*.

One of his cardinals introduced us, saying, 'This is Mr Charlton.' He said, 'Ah yes, the boss.'

> JACK CHARLTON, recalling meeting between the Pope and his Irish squad, World Cup finals, 1990.

Irishman Spotted Playing for Eire

> FANZINE title, *1991*.

Brian Clough

My wife says it stands for Old Big 'Ead.

CLOUGH, Nottingham Forest manager, on his OBE, *1991*.

He's been married to Barbara for umpteen years and she's no idea what he's going to do next, so these young footballers have got no chance.

GEOFFREY BOYCOTT, former England cricketer and friend of Clough's, *1991*.

I lied to my grandson over the weekend and told him we had won the Cup. He's still in the stage of speaking Japanese, so he won't understand.

CLOUGH after Forest's FA Cup Final defeat by Spurs, *1991*.

I scored four times in a 5–2 victory [over QPR]. It was the greatest number of goals I had scored in one match and as I walked to the dressing room I felt sure of a great reception from the manager. 'Eh, Chapman!' he shouted. 'When you score a hat-trick you run over to me, not the supporters. I'm the one who signed you!' It was typical Clough. Just when you expect one thing, you get the exact opposite.

LEE CHAPMAN, Leeds and ex-Forest striker, in *More Than a Match: A Player's Story, 1992*.

He's my idol as a manager, but we don't communicate. The closest we've come was when he tried to kiss me after a testimonial, but I smelled the after-shave and skipped past him.

NEIL WARNOCK, Notts County manager, *1991*.

He's still the best. I'd like to retire with half of what he has achieved in football and a quarter of his dough.

DAVE BASSETT, Sheffield United manager, after 5–2 win at Forest, 1992.

I've played right back, sweeper and now left back, so I've got a full set of defensive roles. I've a feeling the gaffer is trying to find a position I'm good at.

NIGEL CLOUGH on his father, *1992*.

Brian Clough didn't get too involved in the transfer talks. He put his head round the door, kissed our chairman and told us we could call him Brian, but Roy [Keane] had to call him Mister.

LIAM MCMAHON, former Cobh Ramblers manager, *1991*.

I had long hair when I agreed to join Derby but was told Brian Clough wouldn't stand for that, so I bought a do-it-yourself kit. I made such a mess of it that there was big bald patch on top of my head. Ironically, the first thing they told me to do when I arrived was to get my hair cut.

DON O'RIORDAN, veteran Notts County midfielder, *1991*.

They say he rules by fear but you don't last as long as that by frightening people. Sure he upsets his players by telling a few home truths. But he also brings a lot of pleasure to his team because they are allowed to play and enjoy their football.

> DAVID PLEAT, Luton manager, *1991*.

I've played under Bill Shankly and Bob Paisley and Clough is a better manager than both of them. As a manager there's no limit to my respect for him, but as a man he's not my cup of tea. I once told him I'd never be caught standing at a bar having a drink with him. He said I shouldn't worry because the feeling was mutual.

> LARRY LLOYD, former Forest defender, *1991*.

My knees are aching and I've got a new set of false teeth which don't fit. I can't even sign a little lad's autograph book without my reading glasses and even my grandchildren don't like me.

> CLOUGH, *1991*.

On a Saturday he'd waltz down to the dressing room at twenty to three and put a football down in the middle of the room and say: 'Right, this is your best friend. This is what we play with.'

> DARREN WASSALL, Derby and former Forest defender, *1993*.

Who will take his place over the next 10 years? Plastic people, no doubt.

> JACK CHARLTON, Republic of Ireland manager, on Clough's sudden retirement, *1993*.

Like all the great dictators, from de Gaulle to Thatcher, he stayed on a little too long.

> GAZZETTA DELLO SPORT, Italian sports newspaper, *1993*.

Brian has got many qualities but I never realised clairvoyance was one of them.

> FRANK CLARK on becoming Forest manager nine years after Clough tipped him to be his successor, *1993*.

Stan Cullis

The night Stan Cullis got the sack
Wolverhampton wandered round in circles
Like a disallowed goal
Looking for a friendly linesman.

> MARTIN HALL, songwriter and poet, on the Wolves manager of the 1950s in 'The Stan Cullis Blues', *1974*.

Kenny Dalglish

Few great footballers make the transition into management. The reason is that great players are normally like soloists in an orchestra. They perform alone and tend to look down on team-mates with lesser ability. That was never Kenny Dalglish. He was like a conductor. He brought other players into play. He understood that not everyone was blessed with the greatest of skill. He had patience both as a player and a manager.

BOB PAISLEY, who bought Dalglish for Liverpool, *1991*.

Ten Modern Labours of Hercules: 1. Make Kenny Dalglish laugh uncontrollably.

MAIL ON SUNDAY'S magazine, Journo-lists page, *1990*.

This thing about Kenny being sullen is rubbish. He's got a great sense of humour, as anyone who played with him will tell you. If he appears uncommunicative, it's just that he's understandably wary about certain newspapers.

ALAN HANSEN, former Liverpool captain, after Dalglish's re-emergence with Blackburn, *1992*.

I have no hesitation in saying he was one of the great players of all time, but I can't speak of him in the same terms as a manager. That's not a criticism but he didn't begin the job at the grass roots, start with a Second or Third Division club or build a side from scratch. So there are some doubts.

HOWARD KENDALL, Everton manager, on Dalglish's resignation from Liverpool, *1991*.

I nearly choked on my three Shredded Wheat when I heard of his decision [to resign from Liverpool].

BRIAN CLOUGH, Nottingham Forest manager, *1991*.

He [Dalglish] should have taken a leaf out of Brian Clough's book. Before a big game he'd have a few drinks or go for a walk along the front at Scarborough for some jellied eels.

PETER WITHE, Aston Villa assistant manager, on the news that Dalglish had quit, *1991*.

Reporter: Kenny, do you think you've changed since you left Anfield?
Dalglish: Yes, I didn't wear this suit the last time I was here.

EXCHANGE at press conference following Blackburn's visit to Liverpool, *1992*.

A strangulated Billy Connolly.

MIKE LANGLEY, columnist, *The People, 1980s*.

He's incredibly intense about football. He's the only person I've ever seen come off during a match who's still playing every ball. Normally when players are substituted, you'll see them in the dug-out, winding down. Kenny still kicks and heads everything. That epitomises the man.

ALAN HANSEN, *1992*.

Alex Ferguson

He kicks every ball, feels every tackle. He is a man who shows his emotions.

KEVIN MORAN, Blackburn and ex-Manchester United defender, *1993*.

I don't think I ever saw Alex smile. I don't mean to be nasty about the bloke, but even when United had won games 4–0 he would still have a go at someone for not defending properly or for missing a chance.

NEIL WEBB, Nottingham Forest midfielder, recalling his time at Old Trafford, *1993*.

Fergie and I would also go off after a game for a few pints and run over what went wrong and what went right. He could talk football all night. There is a lot to him as a character and he could be great fun with his little quirks. He was also one for coming out with the strangest of things. A couple of Fergieisms were 'Have you ever seen a Pakistani funeral?' or 'Have you ever seen an Italian with a cold?' You would be left to ponder what he meant.

PAT STANTON, Ferguson's former assistant manager at Aberdeen, in *The Quiet Man, 1989*.

Barry Fry

Perhaps Barry couldn't stand the thought of life at Barnet without Stan.

STANLEY BELLER, Barnet solicitor, on Fry's defection to Southend the day after Stan Flashman's resignation as Barnet chairman, *1993*.

I wanted to be manager of England, but I won't get that job because I swear too much.

FRY, on taking over at Southend, *1993*.

George Graham

I remember George. He was a little bit of a poseur at first, a bit lazy when he played up front, the last one you would have imagined going into management. Different now. He has poseurs for breakfast.

FRANK McLINTOCK, captain of the 1971 Arsenal double side, *1991*.

George is not a listener. He has very definite ideas and won't change them for any-one. Certain players do certain jobs. Full stop. He's very positive, very confident. He knows what he wants and he insists on getting it . . . . His preparation for matches is very good. Where he is not so good is when it comes to man-manage-ment, and the one-to-one relationships.

MARTIN HAYES, Swansea and former Arsenal player, *1993*.

It's as though a big noose has been lifted from round my neck, and at last I've found the freedom to play football the way I believe it should be played. George overdid the long ball and didn't want us to play in midfield any more. What he wanted was for someone to sit in front of the back four and dash between the penalty boxes, hardly ever seeing the ball.

MICHAEL THOMAS, Liverpool and former Arsenal midfielder, in an article for which the FA ruled him guilty of bringing the game into disrepute, *1992*.

I admit I am single-minded. I think all of the great football managers have been sin-gle-minded.

GRAHAM, on the Arsenal players' nicknames for him – 'Ayatollah' and 'Gadaffi', *1991*.

Bobby Gould

Bobby Gould thinks I'm trying to stab him in the back. In fact I'm right behind him.

STUART PEARSON, West Brom coach, suspended by manager Gould, *1992*.

Joe Jordan

He has a ration book of words and he doesn't want to use them all up at the one time. . . . He has just given me a row at the bottom of his voice.

JOHN COLQUHOUN, Hearts striker, on his taciturn manager, *1991*.

Kevin Keegan

You're just another punter as far as I'm concerned.

JACK WHITE, Southampton car park steward, refusing Keegan admission to Southampton's Zenith Cup match with West Ham, *1992*.

God on the Tyne

FHM magazine headline, *1993*.

Howard Kendall

David Bowie can't play at Maine Road because he's never played for Everton.

JOKE in Manchester after Kendall, the former Everton manager, signed five ex-Everton players for City at time of Bowie's stadium tour, *1990*.

Howard Kendall worked things out there very quickly. Good luck to him for seeing the problems before I did. It's a club where you can be the world's greatest and the world's worst within a few days.

> MEL MACHIN, former City manager, on his successor's defection back to Everton, *1990*.

When you talk about Manchester City you are talking about a love affair. With Everton you are talking about a marriage.

> KENDALL explaining his return to Goodison Park, *1990*.

There will not be time for a honeymoon. There is too much work to be done in the house.

> ANDY GRAY, former Everton striker, on Kendall's return to Everton, *1990*.

Jim McLean

[He has] a psychic ability to discern the profile of the complete footballer disguised within the gangly frame of a half-formed adolescent.

> RODDY FORSYTH, author, on the veteran Dundee United manager in *The Only Game: The Scots and World Football, 1990*.

McLean has not been unduly touched by modern fashion. He is the kind of manager who thinks players should be dropped for wearing after-shave. And quite right too.

> STUART COSGROVE, author, in *Hampden Babylon: Sex and Scandal in Scottish Football,1991*.

Sir Alf Ramsey

On the one hand, Alf [Ramsey] had Geoff [Hurst] and Roger [Hunt] who could be relied upon to sweat cobs, and on the other Jimmy Greaves, a fantastic finisher but a moderate team player. Alf did what he thought was best for the team. Mind you, if we'd lost, he'd have been condemned for the rest of his days.

> BOBBY CHARLTON, looking back to the England manager's dilemma before the 1966 World Cup Final, *1991*.

Don Revie

He was a manager who was fatally flawed. He functioned only in the perfect environment, one he could fashion himself. Outside that charmed environment, he was less than ordinary and suddenly couldn't manage.

> MANAGEMENT WEEK magazine, reflecting on Revie's transition from Leeds to England manager, *1991*.

If he had one chink in his armour it was that he probably paid teams far more respect than they deserved. He should have just told us certain points and then told us to go out and beat 'em. Just left it to us.

NORMAN HUNTER, ex-Leeds defender, in *An Alternative History of Leeds United, 1991*.

Bruce Rioch

When Rioch came to Millwall we were depressed and miserable. He's done a brilliant job of turning it all around. Now we're miserable and depressed.

DANNY BAKER, presenter of Radio 5 phone-in *606* and Millwall fan, *1992*.

Bobby Robson

I'm glad we didn't win the World Cup, because if we had there would have been pressure for Bobby Robson to stay on, and he's not my type of manager. I wouldn't want to work with him.

PETER SWALES, taking over as chairman of the FA international committee after the World Cup, *1990*.

Today newspaper, having branded Bobby Robson a liar, a cheat and a traitor, continues an editorial comment by saying: 'In previous centuries, a man who committed such treachery would have been sent to the Tower.' In any century, someone who thinks that is a legitimate allusion in a piece about a football manager changing his job should be sent to a padded cell.

HUGH MCILVANNEY, sports writer, *The Observer*, when Robson announced he would be joining PSV Eindhoven after the World Cup finals, *1990*.

Eighteen years as a professional player in Framham and West Bromwitch Albion . . a manager for Ibswich . . . and England's managing job after the World Cup finals in Spain when Mr Wood Green retired [*sic*].

EGYPTIAN GAZETTE profile, *1989*.

Andy Roxburgh

Can you believe my luck? Scotland are in the World Cup finals and the guy who's in charge wears a wig and has a nose that could cut a wedding cake.

CRAIG BROWN, Scotland assistant manager, teasing his boss, *1990*.

People keep portraying me as a pragmatist and a tactician. I'm not – I'm a supporter, a Scotland fan. If Craig [Brown, assistant manager] and I weren't in charge of the team we'd be on the terracing. I'm a victim of my own emotions, just like anyone else. When we scored the winner against Cyprus, we were dancing round the track. It's not the way I like to behave but it was an emotional moment.

ROXBURGH, Scotland coach, *1990*.

86

Roxburgh's a ned. Good on preparation, crap on football.

TERRY BUTCHER, **Rangers and England defender, in Pete Davies,** *All Played Out: The Full Story of Italia '90, 1990.*

Joe Royle

Much as I like Joe Royle and respect him as a manager, I can't take the authorities seriously if they pick a man who has never managed higher than the Second Division, and leave me out.

TERRY VENABLES, Spurs manager, on the FA's short-list for the England manager's job, *1990.*

At the time, the fee was too much money, but then it always is when you buy a player off Joe Royle.

RON ATKINSON, Aston Villa manager, recalling £1.7 million Earl Barrett deal, *1993.*

Jim Ryan

The manager has had a very difficult job and in the circumstances he has done it well.

PETER NELKIN, Luton chairman, after the club avoided relegation on the last day of the season, *1991.*

You don't take a decision to sack a manager on a whim, but Jim wasn't going to change and neither was I.

NELKIN, sacking Ryan 48 hours later.

Ron Saunders

Saunders: Giving the boys the usual load of old rubbish, Ron?
Ron Atkinson: Yes, Ron. I was just telling them what a good manager you are.

EXCHANGE at Atkinson press conference after match between their clubs, *1982*.

Bill Shankly

I'm glad he's not here now. He would have been devastated.

NESSIE SHANKLY, widow of Bill, on Liverpool's decline, *1993*.

Peter Shilton

Peter Shilton would not know a footballer if he saw one. All he has ever been interested in is getting enough players back to protect his selfish hide.

ALAN HUDSON, ex-England midfielder, on his former Stoke team-mate's managerial ambitions in *Call Me a Player*, an unpublished autobiography, *1991*.

Jim Smith

Bugger Cloughie, what about me? I've never won the Cup either, you know.

JIM SMITH, Portsmouth manager, after his side beat Forest 1–0 in the FA Cup sixth round, *1992*.

Walter Smith

Smith admits he is rarely at home of an evening and that his wife and family see him mainly in transit. His idea of relaxation is to pop in to watch Dumbarton reserves.

BRIAN MEEK, columnist, on the Rangers manager in the *Glasgow Herald, 1991*.

It always gets back to the same question for me. Could a former electrician from Carmyle win the European Cup?

SMITH, Rangers manager, *1993*.

Graeme Souness

I didn't go to Scotland to risk breaking other players' legs. I'm very much against this style . . . . I'm expecting a very hot reception when I get back. I think I will be fired.

JAN BARTRAM, Rangers' Danish defender, criticising the Souness style in a Copenhagen newspaper, *1988*.

The gaffer makes everyone sit down and then goes through his comments on the first half. 'Right, you bastards,' he says, or sometimes stronger if we're not playing well.

TERRY BUTCHER, Rangers and England defender, in *Both Sides of the Border, 1987*.

Would you leave your home like that?

AGGIE MOFFAT, St Johnstone tea-lady, to Souness after Rangers' manager allegedly overturned a tea urn in a fit of temper, *1990*.

He went into the referee's room at half-time, and I don't think it was for a cup of tea.

NEIL WARNOCK, Notts County manager, after Souness allegedly put pressure on referee to give Liverpool match-winning penalty, *1991*.

I know that from the first day I took this job at Ibrox there have been those who have said I was merely using Rangers as a stepping stone to so-called bigger things in England.

SOUNESS, then Rangers manager, *1988*.

The only way I'll leave Rangers is if I'm sacked.

SOUNESS, *1989*.

The thing that would prove I was successful would be if I still had this job in ten years.

SOUNESS, at Rangers, eight months before joining Liverpool, *1990*.

I'd be very flattered to be offered the Liverpool job but I would never contemplate leaving Ibrox.

SOUNESS, on 18 February *1991*. By 16 April he had succeeded Kenny Dalglish at Anfield.

I believe he is making the biggest mistake of his life.

DAVID MURRAY, Rangers chairman, *1991*.

He's a vain bastard. I thought he was going to tell me he was having another nose job.

> PHIL BOERSMA, Liverpool assistant manager, after Souness informed him he was going to undergo heart surgery, *1992*.

If you think Liverpool is a danger to your health, try managing Barnet.

> BARRY FRY, Barnet manager, who had suffered two heart attacks, *1992*.

It is difficult to imagine the new polished image of soccer they keep talking about when the manager of one of our most respected teams is pictured on the front page of a tabloid paper eating his girlfriend . . . . What he did was so crass, so insensitive and so plain bloody silly that he must still have been under the influence of the anaesthetic when the pictures were taken.

> MICHAEL PARKINSON, columnist, *Daily Telegraph*, when the hospitalised Liverpool manager was shown kissing his girlfriend on the anniversary of the Hillsborough disaster, *1992*.

He has accepted the board's recommendation that it is inappropriate for the manager of Liverpool to enter into exclusive arrangements with any section of the media.

> PETER ROBINSON, Liverpool chief executive, after story of Souness' heart bypass op appeared in *The Sun* amid outrage on Merseyside, *1992*.

As a person Souness is incredibly arrogant. You could never have a joke with him, especially not a rude one like you'd have with a mate.

> GLENN HYSEN, Liverpool defender, on how Souness 'destroyed the spirit' at Anfield, *1992*.

Liverpool's players emerge from their dressing room. 'Clear head, clear head, clear head,' Souness demands of each player in turn as he pats them on the back of their skulls with a force that seems detrimental to his object.

> IAN RIDLEY, author, *Season in the Cold: A Journey Through English Football, 1992*.

Anybody who plays for me should be a bad loser.

> SOUNESS, after seeing Arsenal take championship from them soon after return to Anfield, *1991*.

I don't remember Souness being a wallflower in his playing days. The side we put out there couldn't maul a church choir.

> ALAN SMITH, assistant manager of Crystal Palace, responding to the Liverpool manager's attack on Palace's 'rough' tactics, *1992*.

Peter Taylor

Peter will now be reminding Bill Shankly of the days Liverpool would play at Derby and lose and telling Don Revie he should have won more trophies with the players at his disposal.

> JOHN SADLER, *Sun* columnist, speaking at Taylor's funeral, *1991*.

Graham Taylor

Graham was never a good player. He was always trying to hit the long ball. He called it his 'escape' ball. I didn't like it and after a while I dropped him . . . . Some-one told me it was the sort of signing that could get me the sack, and six months later that's what I got.

> RON GRAY, former Lincoln manager, recalling the playing background of the England manager, *1992*.

He has this stain on his character from the past.

> BRIAN GLANVILLE, journalist, on Taylor's long-ball regime at Watford, *1990*.

I think he'll succeed, but sometimes he talks too much. When Graham answers a question he goes on and on, he should be more direct. He tries to explain every-thing, and the more he goes on the more he seems to be making excuses. He should be like me and tell people to go away unless you really have something to say.

> JACK CHARLTON, Republic of Ireland manager, *1991*.

He came to watch a Swede play against Denmark, but saw me – an old-fashioned anything-but-continental centre-half. I'm glad he signed me for Villa because he's the best manager I ever had. He's so honest and filled with a love for the game he knows how to instil in players.

> KENT NIELSEN, Denmark and former Aston Villa defender, *1992*.

They can smell the blood of an Englishman, and in this case the Englishman's name is Taylor.

> TAYLOR, as pressure mounted before England's European Championship group match in Poland, *1991*.

The England manager has shown that his style of coaching and playing isn't really what is required for England at the very top flight.

> ALAN MEALE MP, tabling a Commons motion calling for Brian Clough to be made England manager after the European Championship debacle, *1992*.

As a vision of the future it ranks right up there alongside the SDP and the Sinclair C5.

> JOE LOVEJOY, football correspondent, *The Independent*, on Taylor's intention to revert to a more direct game after England's failure, *1992*.

91

Contrary to what some people might think, I am not wanting to see the ball booted aimlessly upfield, but the truly great players hurt the opposition with one devastating pass.

> TAYLOR, elaborating on his 'back to basics' philosophy, *1992*.

Terry Venables

A lot of people seem to think I'm a slippery Cockney boy with a few jokes. It has taken one of the biggest clubs in the world to acknowledge what I can really do – coach.

> TERRY VENABLES, on his success with Barcelona, *1985*.

Fans are very fickle. There is a distinct possibility that three or four games into next season, if we win and the manager becomes a hero, the cruel, harsh reality is that maybe – maybe – Terry is forgotten.

> ALAN SUGAR, Tottenham chairman, on his bid to oust Venables, *1993*.

We're 100 per cent behind Terry. I've even torn down my Amstrad satellite dish and stuck it in the dustbin.

> NEIL RUDDOCK, Spurs captain, after chairman and computer tycoon Sugar tried to sack Venables, *1993*.

Jo Venglos

Jo Venglos was always the favourite at the back of my mind.

> DOUG ELLIS, Aston Villa chairman, *1990*.

He has been a very quick learner. He has even discovered how to swear at his players.

> JOHN WARD, Villa asst manager, on the club's short-lived Czechoslovak appointment, *1990*.

Howard Wilkinson

There are bigger heads than mine in the First Division – Howard Wilkinson springs to mind.

> BRIAN CLOUGH, Nottingham Forest manager, *1991*. Clough later apologised for the remark.

One of his early policies at Wednesday was the introduction of his infamous cross-country runs . . . . The length and regularity of these runs soon became legendary, but their severity eventually became a barrier to the club's attempts to sign new players.

> LEE CHAPMAN, Leeds and ex-Sheffield Wednesday striker, in *More Than a Match: A Player's Story, 1992*.

I'm one of those 20-year, hard graft, overnight successes.

> WILKINSON, on Leeds' championship, *1992*.

CHAPTER 4

The Beautiful Game

STYLE WARS

A symphony has a last bar and a final note, heard a thousand times and never changing. A dance has a concluding step in time with its music, well remembered through practice. Once seen, a play always has the same finale. Beautiful as each may be, after the first experience there is no longer any surprise. Football, on the other hand, contains elements of all these arts, with the endless bonus that each time it can provide a different and often unexpected climax. No one ever knows. There lies its magic!

GEOFFREY GREEN, author, in *Great Moments In Sport, 1972*.

People are always kicking, old or young. Even an unborn child is kicking.

SEPP BLATTER, FIFA secretary-general, *1990*.

I started by kicking a ball around the streets. When I say a ball, sometimes it was a stone, wrapped in banana leaves, or even a grapefruit or a pineapple wrapped in rags. It gives you an advantage when you come to play with a real ball. It seems easier to control.

ROGER MILLA, Cameroon striker, *1991*.

Everything is beautiful. The stadiums are beautiful, the atmosphere is beautiful, the cops on horseback are beautiful. The crowds respect you.

ERIC CANTONA, Leeds' French striker, getting to know English football, *1992*.

When I scored I was so happy I could have kissed everyone, the crowd, every Italian, the whole world.

ROBERTO BAGGIO, Juventus striker, on scoring for Italy, World Cup finals, *1990*.

Football in Britain could not be in a sorrier state. Sport is dying. The future is in culture, spirituality and religion.

ROBERT MAXWELL, millionaire publisher and Derby chairman, *1990*.

Twenty-two grown men chasing a piece of leather round a field.

BERNARD LEVIN, English journalist, describing football in the *New York Times*, after the Hillsborough disaster, *1989*.

To say that these men paid their shillings to watch twenty-two hirelings kick a ball is merely to say that a violin is wood and catgut, that *Hamlet* is so much paper and ink. For a shilling the Bruddersford United AFC offered you Conflict and Art . . . .

J.B. PRIESTLEY in the novel *The Good Companions, 1929.*

Football hasn't changed in 18 months. The ball is not square and they haven't come up with any robots.

DIEGO MARADONA, on returning to football with Seville, *1992.*

Even though we knew it would have put five points on the opinion polls for Mrs Thatcher, we were still cheering for England to win.

JOE ASHTON, Labour MP and Sheffield Wednesday director, during World Cup finals, *1990.*

Football is a damn sight more important than the arty-farty people pushing themselves around the Royal Opera House.

TERRY DICKS, Conservative MP, *1990.*

Football doesn't matter a damn. It used to be a game, now it's become a war.

ANTHONY BEAUMONT-DARK, Conservative MP, 1990.

Football is like war. When the chips are down you need fighters.

IAN BRANFOOT, Southampton manager, *1991.*

I expect them to come out . . . oh dear, I'd better not say fighting, had I?

PETER SHREEVES, Tottenham manager, before Cup Winners' Cup match with Hajduk Split from war-torn Croatia, *1991.*

The players can't concentrate. We are here in Belgrade, while up the road 50 people may die today.

VLADIMIR CVETKOVIC, president of European Cup holders Red Star Belgrade, *1991.*

We're fed up with managers using clichés like 'I want players to die for me.' This is language more appropriate to a war zone than a sporting occasion.

JIM FARRY, Scottish FA secretary, after eight sendings-off on the first day of a new season, *1990.*

If players are not going to die for this club, then I don't want them.

ALEX MILLER, Hibernian manager, after Scottish Cup defeat by Raith Rovers, *1990.*

Our guys are getting murdered twice a week.

ANDY ROXBURGH, Scotland coach, on 'pressures' of British football, *1991.*

If this is what professional football is all about, I'm glad I'm not good enough.

ADIE COWLER, captain of non-League Kingstonian, on FA Cup replay v Peterborough behind closed doors after his goalkeeper had been felled by a coin in the first game, *1992*.

Football has allowed TV and the police to take over.

JIM SMITH, Portsmouth manager, as police restrictions determined that his side's FA Cup semi final v Liverpool had to be decided on penalties, *1992*.

When I was a kid, I'd play soccer and I'd play great and we'd lose. I had a real hard time accepting that. I'm not a good team player.

ANDRE AGASSI, American tennis player, *1990*.

Over the past ten years a myth has grown up that football should in some way strive to be entertaining. Sport is not entertainment. It's an activity for the benefit of the participants. If you run away from that you risk having the wrong pipers calling the tune.

HOWARD WILKINSON, Leeds manager, *1990*.

When people tell me that fans want style and entertainment first I don't believe it. Fans want to win. Style's a bonus.

LOU MACARI, Birmingham manager, *1991*.

We all like to get on the ball and spray it around, but it isn't always possible. Sometimes you have to roll your sleeves up and have a bit of the nitty-gritty.

RAY WILKINS, QPR midfielder, *1990*.

The tempo of the English game is extraordinary whether you are playing a team at the top or at the bottom. In Italy you will find that speed only when you are playing in Milan or Napoli.

GLENN HYSEN, Liverpool and ex-Fiorentina defender, *1989*.

English soccer is the best and I would like to see them win in Sweden. They play for 90 minutes, they try hard and they never lie down unless they are hurt. It is the only soccer you can really watch.

IVAN LENDL, Czechoslovak tennis player, *1992*.

I admire the English mentality because you are so strong, so hard working. But we have talent.

SVEN-GORAN ERIKSON, Benfica's Swedish coach, after his side knocked Arsenal out of the European Cup, *1991*.

This thing about 'not trying' really annoys me. I can get down the wing and beat three men and everyone thinks 'great, terrific'. Next time I get the ball, I start off and the first person beats me. People then say: 'Oh, he's not trying.' This is a common attitude in England – you always have to look as if you're trying. You have to be a hustler to get respect.

JOHN BARNES, Liverpool midfielder, *1990*.

We are treating top-quality athletes like shire horses. You would not ask a racehorse or greyhound to run every four days for 10 months.

STEVE COPPELL, Crystal Palace manager, *1991*.

We don't train in this country. We train at the beginning of the season to get fit – once the season starts, we're a nation of match-play footballers.

BOBBY ROBSON, England manager, in Pete Davies, *All Played Out: The Full Story of Italia '90, 1990*.

I once described football in England as being the working man's ballet. It's more like a clog dance now.

TONY WADDINGTON, former Stoke manager, *1991*.

There is a big problem in football. You have one player who is technique and another who is physique, and the physique wins. Always. Because the ground is 110 metres and you have to run for 90 minutes.

MICHEL PLATINI, France manager, *1992*.

When I began my career as a player with West Brom every club had a playmaker. Now there are hardly any. Most modern midfield players simply hook the ball on and support.

DON HOWE, Coventry and former England coach, *1992*.

It's a shame that players in this country with touch and ability are not encouraged to develop. There are a lot who could have done better. But the public want a frantic game – you hear a bigger cheer for the player who runs 50 yards to make a tackle than the one who brings the ball down, does a few jinks, and releases a clever pass.

PAUL DAVIS, Arsenal and England midfielder, *1991*.

I couldn't possibly have played in the current Arsenal team, because I was one-paced and the game is faster than it was even a few years ago. The players are stronger and more committed. To survive without pace these days – and I'm talking about being creative – you need the skills of a Glenn Hoddle or a Liam Brady.

GEORGE GRAHAM, Arsenal manager and member of the club's double-winning side of 20 years earlier, *1991*.

People try to tell you Stanley Matthews wouldn't get a kick these days but don't you believe it. Nobody succeeded in booting Stan into the crowd because the ball was laid off quickly until he got the upper hand. [He had] the skill and confidence to operate in confined spaces and get past people. Where are the players today who can do this? John Barnes and Mark Walters, young Ryan Giggs? There aren't many.

VIC BUCKINGHAM, **former West Brom, Fulham and Barcelona manager,** *1992.*

The first touch by players in English football disappoints me. When I first played for AC Milan, the first 15 minutes of every training session were spent by each player keeping a ball off the ground – by using his head, feet, knee, shoulder. Franco Baresi, the most skilful defender I've played with, worked every day on his touch.

RAY WILKINS, former England captain, after the national team's poor results in the European Championship finals, *1992.*

My strategy has always been the same. I believe that if you have the ball, you should keep it moving. If you don't have it, you should stop it from moving.

ARSENIO IGLESIAS, coach to Deportivo La Coruña, Spanish championship contenders, *1993*.

My philosophy is to play in their half of the field. Get the ball behind them – get the buggers turning, turning, turning. When you've done that enough times, holes are going to open up, and one of our fellas, whoever's nearest, gets to the ball first, and all the rest pile in.

JACK CHARLTON, Republic of Ireland manager, *1988*.

I don't think that people who talk about sophisticated football know what they're talking about. To me, the more shots you can get and the more times you can threaten the opposition 'keeper the better chance you've got of winning a game. Is that any different at international level than on a Sunday park? I happen to believe that it's not.

GRAHAM TAYLOR, England manager, *1991*.

Bloody hell, I'll have to stop that.

TAYLOR, on being told England had put together 13 passes in the build-up to a goal, *1991*.

I don't believe in unnecessary passing. Most countries build from the back, starting with the full-back, through the centre-back, midfield, the full-back, the centre-back and across the line into midfield. And you [reporters] consider *that* is the way to play the game. Well, we don't. I don't. We won't waste time at the back like that, except when we want to take a rest.

JACK CHARLTON, *1990*.

If current trends continue, it is going to be a game of 6 ft 10 in defenders heading the ball back and forth with 6 ft 11 in forwards.

JOHN CARTWRIGHT, former director of the FA National School, *1992*.

If God had meant football to be played in the air he'd have put grass in the sky.

BRIAN CLOUGH, Nottingham Forest manager, *1992*.

End of the Road for The Long-Ball Game

TIMES headline, *1990*.

Somebody sent me that. I must read it sometime. Meanwhile don't forget your tin-helmet on Saturday.

DAVE BASSETT, Sheffield United and ex-Wimbledon manager, on the *Times* article, 1990.

People complain about our long-ball game, but we kick off at 3.00 and by ten past we've usually hit the woodwork twice and forced nine corners. It's exciting to watch.

> DEREK DOOLEY, Sheffield United managing director, *1990*.

They are just another English club. It doesn't make any difference if we're playing Sheffield United or Manchester United. All English teams play the same way.

> RONALD KOEMAN, Barcelona and Holland sweeper, before the European Cup winners' Cup Final, *1991*. Manchester United won 3–1.

They've ended up in England with a game for Mechanical Man.

> RODNEY MARSH, former England forward, *1992*.

The basic principle of football is to win and to score. Otherwise playing would be like working in a factory, always doing the same thing.

> RUUD GULLIT, AC Milan and Holland player, *1991*.

People really have the wrong idea about how the game is played in Germany. They reckon it's 100 mph stuff, performed by muscular athletes who can run all day. Nothing could be further from the truth. The Germans don't play strict man-for-man marking. There's almost an unwritten law which says: 'You let our play-maker play and we'll do the same for you.'

> MURDO MACLEOD, Hibernian and Scotland midfielder, on his Bundesliga experience with Borussia Dortmund, *1992*.

It is standard practice here for players to fall over far too quickly.

> RAINER ZOBEL, Kaiserslautern coach, after a German dive got Sheffield Wednesday's David Hirst sent off in the UEFA Cup, *1992*.

No one [in Italy] is ever late for training, no one goes out when they shouldn't. If anyone turns up late for training it's really frowned upon; you have let yourself and your team-mates down. Once I got caught in a traffic jam at New Year, when I'd been with my family, and I was fined £5000 for being two hours late.

> GRAEME SOUNESS, Liverpool manager and ex-Sampdoria player, *1991*.

The Italians were spitting at my players all through the game, but they were doing that against the Leeds team I played for 20 years ago.

> TERRY COOPER, Birmingham manager, after Anglo-Italian Cup match v Bari, *1992*.

Italy has lost a unique opportunity. But it would have been unrealistic to expect that a World Cup, which after all is just football, could change Italian society.

> LUCA DI MONTEZEMOLO, head of the Italia '90 organising committee, on building delays and corruption scandals before the World Cup, *1990*.

There is a mafia even in the soccer world. The penalty didn't exist. It was given to let the Germans win.

> DIEGO MARADONA, after Argentina's 1–0 defeat by West Germany in the World Cup Final, *1990*.

You're done – I'll have you shot.

> SALVATORE SCHILLACI, Juventus striker, to Fabio Poli after the Bologna player had slapped his face, *1990*.

He kept complaining about it, but we kept him on for a while because we thought it would wear off.

> GEORGE GRAHAM, Arsenal manager, on Anders Limpar, who sustained a broken jaw and three cracked teeth in a match, *1992*.

It's spreading over his face again.

> TERRY BUTCHER, Coventry player-manager, on Robert Rosario's second nose-break in three days, *1991*.

I never thought of taking him off, even with a broken nose. They're nothing. I tried to get one throughout my career because it adds character to your face.

> GEORGE GRAHAM, Arsenal manager, after broken-nose victim Andy Linighan scored FA Cup final winner, *1993*.

I was faced with a stark choice. I had to decide whether to avoid upsetting referees or to see whether I was free over Christmas to visit Gary Blissett in jail.

> GRAHAM KELLY, FA chief executive, after telling a court that an elbow challenge by Brentford's Blissett in the face of Torquay's John Uzzell could be seen '200 times a week', *1992*.

Clubs like ours spend an enormous amount of time, effort and money trying to attract the general public to football, and he's given them the impression that it's the equivalent of a bar-room brawl.

> MIKE BATESON, Torquay chairman, on Kelly's evidence, *1992*.

Kelly's remarks that he could watch four games a week and see 200 such tackles was the most ludicrous statement I have ever heard. It is almost an encouragement to players to behave recklessly.

> BATESON, as above.

It's tough on the lad but that is a sign of a good centre-half. All the best ones have broken noses and cut eyes.

> IAN BRANFOOT, Southampton manager, after Richard Hall broke his nose, *1992*.

Which is worse, a flare-up lasting 18 seconds or a team with a bad disciplinary record all season which has kicked its way constantly to points?

MARTIN EDWARDS, Manchester United chief executive, on hefty fine and deduction of points after brawl in match v Arsenal, *1990*.

Please cool it – we haven't got anyone scripted for a broken leg.

GRAHAM COLE, television 'cop', at charity match between a TV team and Tottenham Police as the boots began to fly, *1990*.

Our lads are very competitive.

TOTTENHAM POLICE spokesman.

There are too many hammer-throwers in the Scottish League. I sign a world-class player and have him put out of action after a game and a bit. The League is too tough.

GRAEME SOUNESS, Rangers manager, after injury to Oleg Kuznetsov, *1990*.

It is the first time, after a match, that we've had to replace divots in the players.

RON ATKINSON, Manchester United manager, after European tie against a rugged Valencia side, *1982*.

Shin pads are so light these days – they're not the big paperbacks we used to use.

ATKINSON, by then Sheffield Wednesday manager, *1990*.

The fair play gave me goose pimples. Everyone respected each other. It was beautiful.

SEPP BLATTER, FIFA general-secretary, after West Germany v England World Cup semi-final, *1990*.

I didn't learn a thing from the World Cup.

GEORGE GRAHAM, Arsenal manager, *1990*.

LIFESTYLE FILE

Someone asked me last week if I missed the Villa. I said 'No, I live in one.'

DAVID PLATT on life in Italy with Bari, *1991*.

Take it from me, as a failed footballer, there isn't a better way to earn a living, to be paid for what is a hobby and a passion.

HOWARD WILKINSON, Leeds manager, to graduates of FA National School, *1992*.

A successful football career used to be about winning things – now it's about how much money you end up with.

> GRAEME SOUNESS, Liverpool manager, in the wake of FA Cup defeat by Bolton, *1993*.

People say the wages are too high, but it's a short career.

> SIR STANLEY MATTHEWS, whose own playing career lasted nearly 40 years, *1987*.

The most sickening own goal I've seen was by Scott Nisbet against Sparta Prague. I could have cried when it went in because we were on really big bonuses.

> JOHN SPENCER, Rangers striker, *1991*.

I used to be reluctant to say what I did for a living if I met people at a dinner or whatever. 'Oh, you're in football' . . . . there was a certain distaste.

> GEORGE GRAHAM, Arsenal manager, on the game's unpopularity in the 1980s, *1990*.

People come here to play football on the one day off they have from work, and sometimes the resentment and frustration they feel about their jobs comes out and they start fighting. Once one of the teams was playing a black British team, and it ended with people stabbing each other.

> LIONEL SARMIETO, sponsor of Perfect Colombia FC in Clapham Common's Liga Latino Americana de Futbal, *1991*.

I'm sick of forking out fines. One Friday I paid out £80 to the Staffs FA. I played on the Saturday and was sent off. I was booked on the Sunday morning and sent off again on the Sunday afternoon. I've never been a dirty player and never broken anyone's leg, but I seem to have acquired a bad reputation.

> JIM PHILLIPS, player-manager of Potteries park team Swallows Nest, bemoaning his disciplinary problems and career record of 21 dismissals, *1989*.

The worst pressure I'm under is my baby crying in the night.

> ALAN SHEARER, Blackburn's £3.3 million striker, playing down the 'pressure' of his price tag, *1992*.

Football takes all my pressures away. The police have got my passport and I'm not allowed to train with the other players, but nothing bothers me out on the field.

> MICKEY THOMAS, Wrexham captain, as club's FA Cup run coincided with his release on bail on currency charges, *1992*.

None of the forwards were as intimidating as those I met playing for Wealdstone. And there was so much free time. I spent afternoons wandering round shops.

> STUART PEARCE, Nottingham Forest captain, on his early days as a full-time professional after working as an electrician, *1992*.

Programme Editor: What would you be if you weren't a footballer?
Mark Flatts: On the dole.

ARSENAL PROGRAMME player questionnaire, *1993.*

If I wasn't playing, I'd be putting slates on roofs back in Ireland. Playing's got to be better than that.

PAUL MCGRATH, Aston Villa defender, *1993.*

Football is not as glamorous as it's made out to be, but it beats most jobs.

LES FERDINAND, QPR striker and former painter and decorator, on selection for England, *1992.*

People keep asking me about the sun and the sand. Sure, they'll all want to come and stay with me, but I'm not here for a holiday. They can go to the beach – I'll be working.

DAVID PLATT, after his £5.5 million move from Aston Villa to Bari, *1991.*

You'll no doubt have moments of doubt and be tempted to go to the manager for advice. I remember knocking on the Sheffield Wednesday manager's door. I said, 'Could I have a little bit of your time – I don't know whether I'm coming or going.' 'Wilkinson,' he said, 'you're definitely going.'

HOWARD WILKINSON, Leeds manager, to FA National School graduates, *1992.*

One of the reserves came up to me and said, 'I'm finding it hard – it's the first time I've ever been dropped.' So I said to him: 'Do like Nick Faldo does and work at your game.' Next thing I know he's doing exactly what Nick Faldo does. He's taken up golf.

RON ATKINSON, Aston Villa manager, *1991.*

After we won at West Brom I received 193 calls from assorted media and well wishers the following Monday. I even got a call from my first wife's parents, which surprised me a bit seeing as they hadn't bothered to ring for the previous 15 years since the divorce.

GEOFF CHAPPLE, Woking manager, on the power of the FA Cup, *1992.*

My Dad's been nagging me to score. This will keep him off my back for a week or two.

PAT NEVIN, Everton and Scotland winger, after scoring twice v Arsenal, *1989.*

They said if I was unsure I needed only to look out over the Bosphorus and that would make up my mind. I told them that I had recently looked out over the Clyde and that convinced me that I couldn't go through with it.

NEVIN, on why he turned down a Turkish club to join Tranmere, *1992.*

I'm sure I won't cry. I'm supposed to be a big, aggressive, macho centre-forward. Tears wouldn't do my street cred any good. But you never know.

GARRY THOMPSON, Crystal Palace striker, ruled out of the FA Cup Final because he was Cup-tied, *1990.*

It isn't as prestigious as it was. It used to be on a par with footballers, all the players liked to be pictured with Page Three girls. I think they think it's a bit downmarket now.

CORINNE RUSSELL, announcing her retirement as a topless model, *1990.*

If you'd given me a choice of beating four men and smashing in a goal from 30 yards against Liverpool or going to bed with Miss World it would have been a difficult choice. Luckily, I had both. It's just that you do one of those things in front of 50,000 people.

GEORGE BEST, *1991.*

My players have asked me for the home numbers of the Italian lads.

BOBBY GOULD, Wimbledon manager, after Italy's management put a ban on sex until the team were out of the World Cup finals, *1990.*

The average English footballer could not tell the difference between an attractive woman and a corner flag.

WALTER ZENGA, Italy's goalkeeper, responding to Gould, *1990.*

I've nothing against letting the wives into the team camp. Love is good for footballers as long as it is not at half-time.

RICHARD MÖLLER NIELSEN, Denmark manager, European Championship finals, *1992.*

Today is the day for meeting the wives. Footballers are people and, if a man is in discomfort for a long time, it can affect his work.

VALERI NEPOMNIACHI, Cameroon's Russian coach, World Cup finals, *1990.*

It's very important for the players to reintroduce themselves to their wives as husbands should do after having been away for some time.

GRAHAM TAYLOR, England manager, taking his squad home from Finland a week before the European Championship finals instead of going on to Sweden, *1992.*

I simply can't imagine that gay people are able to play football. They would not be hard enough for professional soccer.

PAUL STEINER, Cologne and Germany defender, *1991.*

I would say that more than 25 per cent of football is gay. It's got to be higher than average. It is a very physical, closed world, a man's world, and you form deep bonds with people you hardly know.

JUSTIN FASHANU, Torquay striker, self-confessed bisexual and born-again Christian, *1992*.

In football, finding religion is considered as bad as being gay – if not worse. John Robertson [former Forest team-mate] started calling me Brother Justin.

JUSTIN FASHANU, *1990*.

I don't want my players playing for England because when they come back all they want is big wages, sponsored cars, a big house, Page Three birds, ecstasy and cocaine. I'm happy they don't know about all that.

DAVE BASSETT, Sheffield United manager, *1990*.

Caniggia won't be the last. When I went to the South American Championship in 1977, from a squad of 30 players 20 were on drugs.

CARLOS BILARDO, former Argentina manager, on Claudio Caniggia's positive cocaine test, *1993*.

English players don't have the right image for us. In Japan, they are known for drinking too much, fighting among themselves and being discourteous.

TSUNEO ITO, Japanese FA official, after Grampus Eight's signing of Gary Lineker, *1991*.

I don't smoke or drink, but I will make an exception if we win a trophy. I'll go back into the dressing room and get blootered.

FREDDY VAN DER HOORN, Dundee United's Dutch defender, *1990*.

Any professional sportsman who regularly drinks eight or ten pints in an evening is never going to get very far.

MIKE BATESON, Torquay chairman, threatening to sack six players who reportedly drank around ten pints an evening, *1991*.

Even after a skinful, I don't have a hangover and can still be up with the others.

BRYAN ROBSON, former England captain, on reports that he was a heavy drinker, 1990.

I don't go where people are enjoying themselves and alcohol is flowing freely. I made that vow 13 years ago.

JIMMY GREAVES, TV pundit, ex-England striker and alcoholic, on why he did not attend the reunion of the 1966 World Cup-winning squad, *1991*.

Alcohol controls me. Alcohol is a disease and has nothing to do with personality. I never go a day without thinking about drinking.

GEORGE BEST, *1990.*

Alcohol isn't part of their lifestyle [in Italy]. They work on the principle that your body's a machine, you drain that machine, now you've got to put back into your system whatever is good for that machine. And the one thing you don't fill it with is alcohol.

GRAEME SOUNESS, Liverpool manager and ex-Sampdoria player, *1991.*

If I had my time again I would not do anything different in football. But knowing what I do know, I would never open a pub.

GERD MULLER, former West Germany striker, on being admitted to a clinic for alcoholics, *1991.*

We'll still be happy if we lose – it's on at the same time as the Beer Festival.

NIAL O'MAHONY, Cork City manager, on his team's chances in second leg of UEFA Cup tie v Bayern Munich, *1991.* Cork lost 2–0.

The players will do a training session to run off their Christmas turkey and pub [*sic*] before we set off for an overnight stay.

JOHN RUDGE, Port Vale manager, programme column, *1990.*

Black Death Vodka have sponsored the European Squash Championships with no ill-effects.

COMPANY spokesman after the Football League objected to their sponsoring Scarborough, *1990.*

We really wanted a slogan that said 'Drink Beer, Smoke Tabs' – I reckon that would look dead good on a football kit, but I doubt whether the FA would have approved.

GRAHAM DURY, co-editor of the 'adult' comic *Viz*, on sponsoring Blyth Spartans, *1992.*

After the World Cup I went into McDonald's in Crewe with a friend, not knowing how things had changed. All these people were coming up and asking for my autograph. My cheeseburger went cold.

DAVID PLATT on his new-found fame, *1990.*

They got me for a cup of tea and a couple of pies.

JOHN MARTIN, Airdrie goalkeeper, on his transfer 'fee' from Tranent Juniors, *1992.*

In Italy you couldn't eat bananas and ice cream. In England they don't care what you eat – only what you say.

ANDERS LIMPAR, Arsenal and former Cremonese winger, *1990.*

It's hard work trying to find someone else with my taste in music. There aren't many of us around. When I get on the team coach and play my tapes, they are howled and booed off. They [the other players] all like the middle-of-the-road stuff, but that gives me a headache.

> STUART PEARCE on his passion for punk rock, *1992*. Pearce nominated The Stranglers as his favourite group and the Sex Pistols' 'Anarchy in the UK' as his best song.

I don't like U2, that's rebel music, Southern Irish. And Simple Minds – I found out that Jim Kerr [the vocalist] was a Celtic supporter, so all my Simple Minds tapes, they went out of the window. Celtic, you hate 'em so much . . . .

> TERRY BUTCHER, Rangers and England defender, in Pete Davies, *All Played Out: The Full Story of Italia '90, 1990.*

When the England team was travelling you always knew which hotel room Dave Watson was in because he took with him a radio-cassette player with big speakers and you could usually hear the music all the way down the corridor. His favourite group was Status Quo.

> TREVOR BROOKING, former England midfielder, in *100 Great British Footballers, 1988.*

It's obtaining goals by menaces. Showing violent films before a match is like throwing the lads red meat. Watching blood and guts arouses aggression, and when they go on the pitch they won't be too squeamish about putting the boot in. If they had sex films to watch they might become too relaxed.

> DAVID LEWIS, psychologist, on the FA's selection of 50 videos to take to the World Cup, *1990.*

In every squad of 20 players there's going to be the one who hates blacks, foreigners. He don't know why. He just hates 'em.

> VINNIE JONES, Chelsea midfielder, on racism in football, *1991.*

They arrived at the stadium in cars where previously they had come by bus or tube, they dined in smart Chinese restaurants instead of caffs, they wore slick clothes and had haircuts like Perry Como or Jack Kennedy. They were as well groomed as male fashion models and their dressing rooms reeked of after-shave lotion.

> JOHN MOYNIHAN, author, on the changing lifestyle of footballers in the early 1960s, *Soccer Syndrome, 1966.*

Cut-out-and-keep guide to success in modern game

Age 15: Appoint Headmaster as your first agent.
Age 17: Sign pro forms for Bigmoney FC.
Age 18: Buy first set of golf clubs. Make first-team debut. Report says 'Covered every blade of grass'. Qualcast sponsor you.

Age 22: Called into England squad. 'His long throws could win us World Cup,' claims England manager. Debut v Tibet, 0–0 draw. Long throw noted favourably by Dalai Lama.

Age 26: Fanzine named after your now-legendary throw-ins: *Eddie's Got a Long One*

Age 29: On *Desert Island Discs* choose seven Dire Straits records and 'Lady in Red' by Chris de Burgh.

Age 33: Appointed player-manager of local team. Buy first sheepskin coat.

SATURDAY AFTERNOON & SUNDAY MORNING, Nottingham-based fanzine, *1991*.

Sometimes, driving home from a game, you do wonder if you are getting old. But I always remember what Kenny Dalglish once told me: never forget that football made you feel knackered when you were 17.

GORDON STRACHAN, Leeds midfielder, in *An Autobiography, 1992*.

I'm frightened to stop because there can be no life as enjoyable as this.

STRACHAN, on a footballer's life at 35, *1992*.

If someone told me I could swap the football career I've had for a life without Parkinson's disease, I wouldn't change a thing.

RAY KENNEDY, former Arsenal, Liverpool and England player, *1992*.

CHAPTER 5

Philosophers Utd

Rimbaud wanted to write about everything, to seek flashes of inspiration, to enjoy different ideas and live with different philosophies. He had the spontaneity of a child, and I believe in that. He was the pioneer, but the torch he lit was picked up by others, like Jim Morrison, and I believe that even in football, I should live as instinctively as that.

ERIC CANTONA, Manchester United striker, *1993.*

One minute you can be riding on the crest of a wave in this game and the next minute you can be down. It's a funny old game, it's a great leveller, and you can't get too cock-a-hoop about things. I know it's an old cliché, but you've got to take each game as it comes and keep working at it. You're only as good as your last game, whether you're playing or in management.

BILLY BONDS, West Ham manager, *1990.*

Opinions in football are very important, especially the opinions of the players. They are closest to the action and it is up to influential players to make their views known.

RICHARD GOUGH, Rangers and Scotland captain, *1992.*

I'd rather be a footballer than an existentialist.

ROBERT SMITH, vocalist with rock group The Cure, *1991.*

That's great. Tell him he's Pele and get him back on.

JOHN LAMBIE, Partick Thistle manager, on being told that concussed striker Colin McGlashan did not know who he was, *1993.*

Football is all about football.

BOBBY GOULD, Coventry manager, *1992.*

Football is a game – the language it don't matter as long as you run your bollocks off.

DANNY BERGARA, Stockport's Uruguayan-born Spanish-speaking manager, *1991.*

Having players you've sold come back and score against you is what football is all about.

ALEX FERGUSON, Manchester United manager, *1992*.

Professional football is an interval between real life and real life.

TONY AGANA, Sheffield United striker, *1990*.

Professional and amateur football have as much in common as a strawberry milk-shake and a skyscraper.

TONI SCHUMACHER, West Germany goalkeeper, in *Blowing the Whistle, 1987*.

If we played like that every week, we wouldn't be so inconsistent.

BRYAN ROBSON, Manchester United captain, *1990*.

If I was still at Ipswich I wouldn't be where I am today.

DALIAN ATKINSON, Aston Villa striker, *1992*.

A few fly bites cannot stop a spirited horse.

JOHN BECK, Cambridge manager, replying to attacks on his team's 'style', *1992*.

We threw caution to the wind and came back from the dead. Well, it is Easter Monday.

GLENN HODDLE, Swindon player-manager, after his team had come from 4–1 down to win 6–4 at Birmingham, *1993*.

The cat's among the pigeons and meanwhile we're stuck in limbo.

BERNIE SLAVEN, Middlesbrough striker, after the departure of manager Colin Todd, *1991*.

I can see the carrot at the end of the tunnel.

STUART PEARCE, England defender, on his chances of recovering from injury to play in the European Championship finals, *1992*.

If we think they will be easy meat we'll end up with egg on our faces.

TERRY DOLAN, Bradford City manager, *1989*.

Ruel Fox is like a bar of soap sometimes. When he's on song it's difficult to nail him down.

DAVE STRINGER, Norwich manager, *1990*.

No one wants to commit hari-kari and sell themselves down the river.

GARY LINEKER, England striker and captain, explaining the dearth of goals at the European Championship finals, *1992*.

The plastic pitch is a red herring.

GRAHAM TAYLOR, Aston Villa manager, after losing FA Cup tie at Oldham, *1990*.

Half the lies about us aren't true.

ANONYMOUS Cambridge player on criticism of the 'new Wimbledon', *1992*.

We feel like we're driving a Mini Metro round a Grand Prix circuit.

JOE ROYLE, Oldham manager, on the difficulty of running a small club in the Premier League, *1993*.

They don't judge Pavarotti by how he sings in the shower; they wait until he is on the stage.

LEO BEENHAKKER, Holland manager, replying to criticism of his team in their World Cup warm-up matches, *1990*.

People said it was going to be a baptism of fire. Well the fire has stopped burning, but we are taking on water.

BOBBY GOULD, West Brom manager, as his new club slipped towards relegation, *1991*.

We were in the driving seat and jumped out for five minutes while they drove us over a cliff.

JOHN KING, Tranmere manager, after 3–2 win v Newcastle, *1991*.

We climbed three mountains then proceeded to throw ourselves off them.

BILLY MCNEILL, Celtic manager, after beating Partizan Belgrade 5–4 but losing on aggregate, *1989*.

He was flapping about like a kipper.

JOHN BARNWELL, Notts County manager, on Nicky Laws' costly handling offences against Tottenham, *1989*.

Some of my defenders think a tackle is something you go fishing with.

BARRY FRY, Barnet manager, after 7–4 defeat by Crewe in first League game, *1991*.

We could have done with half-time not arriving, but you have to have half-time.

GRAHAM TAYLOR, England manager, after defeat by Sweden, *1992*.

From looking like winning it at half-time we let the convict out of jail, and we know what these are like when they get free.

HOWARD WILKINSON, Leeds manager, after a 3–0 defeat by VfB Stuttgart in the European Cup, *1992*.

We had a very constructive discussion at half-time . . . then decided to give it the full bollocks.

> RON ATKINSON, Aston Villa manager, *1993*.

At half-time I told the lads that the only thing you can't repair in life is death.

> DANNY BERGARA, Stockport manager, after his side's second-half fightback had failed to prevent Port Vale winning the Autoglass Trophy, *1993*.

The first goal was a foul, the second was offside and they would never have scored the third if they hadn't got the other two.

> STEVE COPPELL, Crystal Palace manager, after defeat by Liverpool, *1991*.

We had enough chances to win this game. In fact, we did win it.

> ALEX SMITH, Aberdeen manager, *1991*.

There are 0–0 draws and 0–0 draws – and this was a 0–0 draw.

> JOHN SILLETT, Coventry manager, *1989*.

It was a game of two halves, and we were rubbish in both of them.

> BRIAN HORTON, Oxford manager, *1990*.

My strikers couldn't hit a donkey's arse with a frying pan.

> DAVE BASSETT, Sheffield United manager, *1991*.

At least we were consistent – useless in defence, useless in midfield and crap up front.

> RON ATKINSON, Aston Villa manager, after 3–0 defeat at Coventry, *1992*.

I am not in the picture, so I didn't expect to be in the photo.

> ROY AITKEN, Newcastle midfielder, after being told to stay away from the club's pre-season photocall, *1991*.

There was a lot of diving. Armstrong, Gates and Bennett looked as if they'd been training in a swimming pool all week.

> JIM SMITH, Newcastle manager, after bitter play-off v Sunderland, *1990*.

It was a mistake as big as a house.

> RENE HIGUITA, Colombia goalkeeper, after his error gifted a goal to Cameroon's Roger Milla, World Cup finals, *1990*.

He had no repartee with the fans.

> PETER SWALES, Manchester City chairman, after sacking Mel Machin as manager, *1989*.

We're a First Division club in every sense of the word.

> NAT LOFTHOUSE, President of Third Division Bolton, *1992*.

You've got to kill the bull, or you haven't done nowt.

> DANNY BERGARA, Stockport's Uruguayan manager, using a bull-fighting analogy, *1992*.

Like shooting wee ducks at a fairground to try and win a prize.

> ALEX SMITH, Aberdeen manager, on their penalty shoot-out victory in the Scottish Cup Final, *1990*.

Our back four was at sixes and sevens.

> RON ATKINSON, Aston Villa manager, *1992*.

Chester made it very difficult for us by having two men sent off.

> JOHN DOCHERTY, Bradford City manager, *1990*.

The Pope was smaller than I expected, but only in size.

> JACK CHARLTON, Republic of Ireland manager, after taking his squad to the Vatican, World Cup finals, *1990*.

We need to go into our next match with all guns blazing – like the charge of the Light Brigade.

> ANDY ROXBURGH, Scotland manager, after defeat in Romania, *1991*.

I'm here to say goodbye – maybe not goodbye but farewell.

> BOBBY ROBSON, leaving the England managership, *1990*.

We'll be all right in the League. We've just got to treat each game as a Cup-tie.

> FRANK STAPLETON, Manchester United striker, after they had been knocked out of the main cups by Oxford and Bournemouth respectively, *1984*.

If you take liberties with any opposition, they will pull your trousers down.

> BILLY BONDS, West Ham manager, programme column, *1991*.

In footballing terms, two of them are not even on solids.

> RAY MATTHIAS, Wigan manager, on his young back four (average age 19), *1989*.

We've gone back to the Sermon on the Mount to read how He did it with five loaves and two fishes.

> ALEC KING, Sunderland commercial manager, on the problems of allocating FA Cup Final tickets, *1992*.

It is a champagne sponsorship that will bring a bubble, sparkle and zest to our cup.

> GORDON MCKEAG, Football League President, on Coca-Cola's sponsorship of the League Cup, *1992.*

If you can't join them, beat them.

> UFFE ELKMANN-JENSEN, Danish Foreign Minister, when his country won the European Championship soon after rejecting the Maastricht Treaty, *1992.*

It would have taken a brave man not to wear brown pants after looking at their teamsheet and then at ours.

> NEIL WARNOCK, Notts County manager, after First Division match against Arsenal, *1991.*

I feel like Corky the Cat who has just been run over by a steamroller, got up and had someone punch him in the stomach.

> HOWARD WILKINSON, Leeds manager, after FA Cup defeat by Arsenal, *1993.*

There's more ice down here than sunk the Bismarck.

> GERRY FRANCIS, QPR manager, as injuries at the club proliferated, *1991.*

I hope you were as delighted as I was last weekend when Nelson Mandela was freed from a South African jail. But what I hadn't bargained for was the fact that his release was going to cut across the start of our Littlewoods Cup Final.

> BRIAN CLOUGH, Nottingham Forest manager, programme column, *1990.*

The [FA] Cup touches so many people. It's a fair bet that, by the end of today, players you have never heard of will be household names – like that fellow who scored for Sutton United against Coventry City last season.

> BOBBY CAMPBELL, Chelsea manager, programme column, *1990.*

So once more the cruel carousel of time has cantered along its cyclic way and we find ourselves not quite ripe and ready for the start of another ride on football's merry-go-round.

> BOHEMIANS FC (Dublin) programme editorial at start of season, *1990.*

I would tell you what it means if I could translate it.

> GEORGE GRAHAM, Arsenal manager, on an FA directive about the professional foul, *1991.*

I've become something of a bookworm.

> JOHN FASHANU, Wimbledon striker, appointed to the Government Working Party on PE in schools, *1990.*

Further to your recent letter I am sorry that we cannot help you with your search for academics. In fact two of the back four cannot read.

> JOE ROYLE, Oldham manager, replying to journalist researching a feature on footballers with degrees, *1987*.

Happiest memory: collecting my English degree from Swansea University.

> MIKE HOOPER, Liverpool goalkeeper, in programme questionnaire, *1992*.

Person you'd most like to meet: Mike Tyson any place, any time.

> VINNIE JONES, Leeds midfielder, in programme questionnaire, *1989*.

Q: Which is your favourite programme on TV?
A: Most nature programmes.
Q: Which programme would you switch off?
A: Soaps and Luton on *Match of the Day*.

> JONES, interviewed in Chelsea programme, *1991*.

If victory has a hundred fathers, defeat is an orphan.

> PETER SHREEVES, Tottenham manager, quoting Italian World War Two politican Galeazzo Ciano before European tie v Feyenoord, *1992*.

Only dead fish swim with the tide.

> JOHN BECK, Cambridge manager, *1991*.

Sometimes we are predictable but out of that predictability we are unpredictable.

> BECK, *1992*.

We are like the old-time miners when the annual Fair Holiday fortnight came round. They would get their wages on Friday morning, but still have a shift to do before they could go on holiday. Our position is the same.

> ALEX SMITH, Aberdeen manager, before championship decider at Rangers when, needing a draw, Aberdeen lost, *1991*.

The trouble with you son is that your brains are all in your head.

> BILL SHANKLY, Liverpool manager, to player, *1960s*.

Life has to be lived forwards, but can only be viewed backwards.

> SLOGAN on Howard Wilkinson's office wall, *1991*.

Being top won't change too many things. It will probably rain tomorrow and the traffic lights will still be red.

> WILKINSON, asked how it felt to be top of the League for the first time in his career, *1991*.

Complacency is a terminal disease. You can't stand still – there is no comfort zone.

WILKINSON, **on why he had left First Division Sheffield Wednesday to manage Second Division Leeds,** *1990.*

It makes you wonder if we should have a traffic cone somewhere on the national flag.

JOE ROYLE, Oldham manager, after successive Saturdays of trouble on the motorways, *1990.*

Most teams get treated for cuts and bruises at half-time. We have our nuts tightened.

CHRIS SOLE, goalkeeper for Roehampton Amputees FC, *1992.*

I'll tell you something – we're a better team than that 'Legover' Warsaw lot they played in the Cup Winners' Cup.

RON ATKINSON, Sheffield Wednesday manager, predicting a hard time for Manchester United in the Rumblelows Cup Final, *1991.* Wednesday won 1–0.

Rotherham reminds me of Bermuda. It's small, so you bump into the same people two or three times a day.

> SHAUN GOATER, Rotherham's Bermudan international striker, *1993*.

It seems we are incapable of playing well until after Christmas, so we are having it before the season starts.

> DAVE BASSETT, Sheffield United manager, organising the club Christmas party in August, *1992*.

It's a great year. We're champions and all political problems are solved. OK, not all political problems are solved.

> JEAN-LUC DEHAENE, Belgian Prime Minister and ardent Club Bruges supporter, *1992*.

Interviewer: Who do you prefer, Rangers or Celtic?
Alfie Conn: Spurs.

> EXCHANGE on *It's Only a Game*, TV documentary about Scottish football, *1986*. Conn played for all three clubs.

Q: Which TV programme would you most like to appear in?
A: *Thunderbirds*. I'd like to fly in Thunderbird II.

> KEVIN KEEN, West Ham midfielder, interviewed in club programme, *1992*.

'Anything you say may be used in Everton against you,' said Harry. And it was.

> JOHN LENNON, of The Beatles, in *In His Own Write, 1964*.

I took a penalty against Chelsea in 1971 and Peter Bonetti, the fucker, he saved it! I wish I'd sent it the other way!

> GEORGE BEST, former Manchester United player, asked by *Esquire* magazine if there was one thing about his life he would like to change, *1991*.

Footballers are no different from human beings.

> GRAHAM TAYLOR, England manager, *1992*.

It was nearly my finest hour, but life is made up of so-nearlies.

> TAYLOR, after England lost a 2–0 lead to draw with Holland, *1993*.

—— CHAPTER 6 ——
Gazza Gazzetta

HOW OTHERS SEE HIM

Literally the most famous and probably the most popular person in Britain today.

TERRY WOGAN, introducing Paul Gascoigne on his BBC TV show, *1990*.

I'm extremely grateful to Gazza and all he's done because at least people are going to be able to spell my name properly.

BAMBER GASCOIGNE, former *University Challenge* presenter, *1990*.

Where is Gascoigne? I must speak with him. He is a dog of war with the face of a child.

GIANNI AGNELLI, Juventus president, on Gascoigne's display v West Germany, World Cup semi-final, *1990*.

Gazza, Daft as a Brush

GASCOIGNE book title, *1989*.

Deft as a brush

SUNDAY CORRESPONDENT headline on Gascoigne feature, *1990*.

Fierce and comic, formidable and vulnerable, urchin-like and waif-like, a strong head and torso with comparatively frail-looking breakable legs, strange-eyed, pink-faced, fair-haired, tense and upright, a priapic monolith in the Mediterranean sun – a marvellous equivocal sight.

KARL MILLER, writer, *London Review of Books, 1990*.

Footballers today have haircuts resembling a hedge, Gazza's intellect and know all the words of *The Birdie Song.*

NOEL SWEENEY, barrister, defending man on charge of grievous bodily harm against Bristol Rovers' striker Devon White, Exeter Crown Court, *1991*.

He has pop-star status – the first footballer with a world superstar image like the heroes of individual sports – racing drivers, tennis players and so on.

LEN LAZARUS, Gascoigne's co-business manager, *1991*.

We've seen nothing like this since The Beatles.

> SHELBOURNE FC STEWARD encountering Gazzamania at a full-house pre-season friendly in Dublin, *1990*.

He is his own best PR, but we always knew he was no Pavarotti. I wouldn't advise him to hang up his boots just yet.

> RAY LAIDLAW, Lindisfarne drummer, on Gascoigne the pop singer as his remake of 'Fog on the Tyne' hit the charts, *1990*.

Keep him away from Diana.

> BUCKINGHAM PALACE official after Gascoigne described Mrs Thatcher as 'nice and cuddly', *1990*.

Did anyone before Paul Gascoigne ever become a national hero and a dead-cert millionaire by crying? Fabulous. Weep and the world weeps with you . . . . Now that he's a recording star, he could really work it into his repertoire. A collaboration with Tears for Fears, why not. An album of weepie classics. 'Crying in the Rain', 'Tears of a Clown', 'It's My Party (And I'll Cry If I Want To)'. After all, as the song says, You Would Cry Too, If It Happened To You.

> SALMAN RUSHDIE, novelist and writer, *Independent on Sunday, 1990*.

GAZZA AND FIANCE IN SPLIT

> THE SUN, front-page headline at height of Iraq crisis, *1990*.

Britain's biggest bore.

> TYNESIDE radio listeners' verdict, New Year's Eve, *1991*. Gascigne topped the poll ahead of Jeremy Beadle and Cilla Black.

He not only makes an idiot of himself but disgraces the whole region.

> NEWCASTLE JOURNAL editorial after Gascoigne was involved in a nightclub incident, *1991*.

Nobody can now use the name Gazza without a licence from his company, Paul Gascoigne Promotions. Put simply, his company owns the right to the use of that name, just as if it were Dick Tracy or Mickey Mouse.

> LEN LAZARUS, Gascoigne's accountant, *1990*.

My schoolmates were calling me Gazza before this lad was born.

> GEORGE GASCOIGNE, 56-year-old Tyneside electrician, reacting to Lazarus's attempt to copyright his nickname, *1990*.

Q: If your house burnt down, what possession would you want to dive in and save? *A*: My Yorkshire terriers, Gazza and Killer.

> OSSIE ARDILES, West Brom manager, in programme questionnaire, *1993*.

Wherever I look now I see Gazza's smiling face; bright, blind-bird eyes, pink piglet skin; mouth permanently ajar, teeth exposed in a curving arc, tongue alert for protrusion.

> LAURA THOMPSON, columnist, *The Times, 1990*.

Q: Do you think Mr Gascoigne is more famous than the Duke of Wellington was in 1815?
A: I have to say I think it's possible.

> EXCHANGE between Mr Justice Harman and Michael Silverleaf, Gazza's counsel, during the player's attempt to stop the publication of an unauthorised biography, *1990*.

Azha's better than Gazza

> INDIAN cricket supporters' banner in honour of their captain, Azharuddin, at Old Trafford Test match, *1990*.

Gazza kept telling me I was rubbish – and that was one of the compliments. Most of the things he said were unrepeatable.

> ROY KEANE, Nottingham Forest midfielder, on Gascoigne's alleged attempts to 'wind him up', *1990*.

If my daughters behaved like that, I'd give them a good smack and send them to their rooms.

> DAVE BASSETT, Sheffield United manager, on Gascoigne's antics on pitch, *1990*.

If he were a Brazilian or an Argentinian you would kiss his shoes.

> ARTHUR COX, Derby manager, after Gascoigne had led Spurs to a 3–0 win over his team, *1990*.

Always seems to be about two stone overweight.

> PROGRAMME pen-picture of Gascoigne, Republic of Ireland v England, *1990*.

I've run out of patience on the question of his attitude and temperament. I want to know for sure. If we are not careful, Paul Gascoigne's going to be like Matt Monro – dead before we appreciate his talent.

> BRIAN CLOUGH, Nottingham Forest manager, advising Bobby Robson to pick Gascoigne for England, pre-World Cup, *1990*.

I thought he would have lasted 90 minutes, but he used up so much energy in the dressing room he knocked himself out. He was nervous, excited. He was wound up and got the players going. He was magnificent. At half-time I couldn't get a word in edgeways.

> TERRY VENABLES, Spurs manager, on Gascoigne's performance in Spurs' 3–1 win v Arsenal, FA Cup semi-final, *1991*.

I've asked our coach driver, if he sees him in the tunnel at Wembley, to try and knock him down. I don't think we'll stop him otherwise.

BRIAN CLOUGH before the FA Cup Final, *1991*.

Outside his door I just froze. I was too scared to go in. But he shouted 'Come in, darling.' He's got a lovely hairy chest and his leg was raised up on a machine to exercise it. He said 'Come over here, darling, and give us a kiss.'

TINA BIRD, Gazza fan, visiting him in hospital after his FA Cup Final injury, *1991*.

The match against the Republic of Ireland is a very big game and we want Paul Gascoigne to be in the right frame of mind for it. If Mr Taylor wants to see Paul for a few days before the match, that can be arranged. It is possible for us to cancel commitments . . . if the England manager has any special requests in relation to the build-up to the Irish game, I will look at them. We are prepared to consider anything that is in the best interests of Paul Gascoigne's football.

MEL STEIN, Gascoigne's adviser, *1991*.

GAZZA AND SEXY MISS WHIPLASH

NEWS OF THE WORLD front-page headline, *1991*.

Gazza can be a right pain in the neck, and very irritating, but you can't help but like him. He's still lovable, even when he does something diabolical.

GARY LINEKER, *1991*.

We were sat down before the match, me and the linesmen, having a cup of tea in the officials' room. The door opened and it was this Newcastle player. This was unusual – players don't usually do that sort of thing. It was Paul Gascoigne, and he'd come for a chat. He talks through all the games. He says something and nothing – half the time he doesn't know himself.

NEIL MIDGLEY, referee, *1991*.

So many players are ill-advised. It's like me signing for a Mickey Mouse record company just because they pay me so many thousand pounds up front. That is not to say that Lazio are a Mickey Mouse club because I would not want to insult them, but if I was a player of Paul Gascoigne's ability, I would want to play for really big clubs. Tottenham are bigger than Lazio.

ELTON JOHN, rock star and former Watford chairman, *1991*.

I love Gazza. He is so funny. I love it when he smells the referee's armpits and the referee can't do anything about it.

FRANCO ZEFFIRELLI, film director and football fan, *1991*.

He'll still do daft things, but overall he'll learn how to handle his career sensibly.

GARY LINEKER predicting Gascoigne's future when he moved to Italy, *1992*.

I wouldn't have thought that Gazza would be very happy in Italy or anywhere else abroad. He is very much an English kind of guy, and the thought that people wouldn't understand his jokes would kill him.

TERRY VENABLES, Spurs manager, on Gazza's proposed transfer, *1991*.

I'm pleased for him but it's like watching your mother-in-law drive off a cliff in your new car.

TERRY VENABLES, Spurs chief executive, when Gazza finally joined Lazio, *1992*.

Paul is a great player and a great professional. I never believed what they told me about his character. He blends with the group, he succeeds in keeping the company happy, but he is also a man who works on the field with great seriousness.

DINO ZOFF, Lazio manager, in Gascoigne's early days with the Roman club, *1992*.

It will be a study on an English yob abroad, though of course I didn't mean that.

TONY LACEY, Penguin Books Editor, commissioning a biography of Gazza by poet Ian Hamilton, *1992*.

For two years we've been trying to eke out results without Gascoigne. You find yourself saying 'Please God, don't let anything else go wrong with him.'

GRAHAM TAYLOR, England manager, after Gascoigne's return to the national team, *1992*.

Paul is more priceless than the crown jewels. England should wrap him up in something special to make sure nothing happens to him because he is so important to the team. He's got to go down as a national treasure.

IAN WRIGHT, Arsenal and England striker, *1992*.

For all the laddish pranks and waggish stunts, the picture is drawn of a vulnerable, suspicious man-child of 25 who is still trying to come to terms with the scope of his talent. If the gods had been less generous, he might well have been content to be the best player in the pub team; supping pints and chasing lasses and pulling daft faces to his heart's content.

PATRICK COLLINS, columnist, *Mail on Sunday, 1992*.

He says what he feels and his language at times leaves you thinking 'oh my God'. That's Gascoigne. The downside helps to make these people what they are – the Gascoignes and the Bothams.

GRAHAM TAYLOR, England manager, after Gazza had said 'Fuck off Norway' on live television, *1992*.

You'll have to excuse Gazza. He's got a very small vocabulary.

LAWRIE MCMENEMY, England's assistant manager, trying to smooth things over with the Norwegians, 1992.

122

It's not as bad as someone talking dirty down the phone to his mistress – will the Queen fine Prince Charles?

> MEL STEIN, Gascoigne's adviser, when Lazio threatened to fine his client for belching into a TV microphone, *1993*.

Comparing Gascoigne with the Phantom of the Opera is to do the Phantom an injustice – he's playing more like Sarah Brightman.

> MARCUS BERKMANN, *Independent on Sunday* columnist, when Gascoigne took to wearing a carbon-fibre mask to protect an injured cheek-bone, *1993*.

Comparing Gascoigne to Pele is like comparing Rolf Harris to Rembrandt.

> RODNEY MARSH, former England striker, *1990*.

The only thing Gazza and I have in common is that we're both white.

> GEORGE BEST, *1990*.

It's difficult to say, but yes.

> BEST, asked if he had been a better player than Gazza, *1991*.

He wears a No. 10 jersey. I thought it was his position, but it turns out to be his IQ.

> BEST, *1992*.

I once said that Gazza's IQ was less than his shirt number and he asked me: 'What's an IQ?'

> BEST, *1993*.

He has a weight problem. He trains hard – that's no problem, but it's not just training. It's how you feed and how you, let us say, 'refuel yourself' between games.

> GRAHAM TAYLOR, England manager, after the 1–1 draw in Poland, *1993*.

I'm not aware that he has a drink problem, nor that he has abused his drinking. Beer is intrinsic to Gascoigne's diet. We accept that he came to us from a different culture. There was no point in changing his habits. The body accustoms itself to drawing from certain foods, and beer has been part of his elementary habit. In moderation it is certainly OK.

> CLAUDIO BARTOLINI, Lazio doctor, replying to Taylor's charge.

THE LAD HIMSELF

I don't want to end up like him.

PAUL GASCOIGNE on George Best, *1990*.

The only time I feel safe now is in the middle of a football pitch. At least there I know I can escape for a couple of hours.

GAZZA on the effects of Gazzamania, *1990*.

Sometimes I feel like doing a runner for a few days and just hiding, taking the phone off the hook.

ON THE price of fame, *1990*.

No, no, no, yes, no.

HIS response to written questions by Italian reporters, World Cup finals, *1990*.

I want to make a lot of money so I don't have to do anything in ten years' time.

ON SIGNING an £800,000 deal to advertise Brut, *1990*.

Sometimes I think I'm playing in the wrong era.

ON BEING targeted by opponents, *1990*.

It gets to something when my mates have got to hide me in the boot of the car to get me in and out of my home and White Hart Lane . . . . What's the use of being famous if you can't go anywhere without being besieged by people, or you can't get to sleep?

ON HIS popularity, post-World Cup, *1990*.

I didn't get it for crying.

ON WINNING the *Sportsview* Personality of the Year award, *1990*.

I am a marked man. Every time I go out there are people coming up to me. I wish I was as big as Frank Bruno, but I'm only 5 ft 9 in.

AFTER his alleged assault of two men in Newcastle upon Tyne, *1991*.

I don't think I swore. If I did it was not at the referee – it was just me swearing.

ON HIS dismissal v Manchester United on New Year's Day, *1991*.

Tackling: Keep your eye on the ball and try and force your opponent into the first move – let him commit himself before you do . . . . Try and come out of the tackle with a bit of style and panache . . . . Always stand up nice and straight, keep your-self solid.

ADVICE in his book *Soccer Skills with Gazza*, published shortly before his own lunging tackle in FA Cup Final which caused his long injury, *1991*.

I went for the ball, played the ball and couldn't help but follow through. I never set out to top anybody. I've watched the replay and it does look much worse than it was; but nobody would have said much about it if it had been anybody apart from me or Vinnie Jones.

EXPLAINING his wild first-minute challenge on Nottingham Forest's Garry Parker in the FA Cup Final, *Gazza's Football Year, 1991*.

I thought he [Gary Charles] was going to take the ball on and I ran too far and totally mistimed the tackle when he was too quick for me. Our instructions were to get stuck in, to be first, to win every tackle. I was determined to follow them to the letter and all I was trying to do was win the ball.

EXONERATING himself for a second reckless tackle in the final, which wrecked his own knee, *Gazza's Football Year, 1991*.

Sue, the tea-lady here, makes such a good lasagne that there's no need to go all the way to Europe.

EXTOLLING the virtues of Tottenham's cooking as Italian clubs began to take an interest, in *Gazza, Daft as a Brush, 1990*.

I've come for a suntan and the challenge. Money has nothing to do with it.

VISITING Italy to discuss move to Lazio, *1991*.

Coping with the language shouldn't be a problem. I can't even speak English yet.

RETURNING after provisionally agreeing the transfer, *1991*.

The only target I had was to prove a few people wrong, like those so-called ex-pros who knock you down in the papers for a few bob.

AFTER PASSING a fitness test to allow his transfer to Lazio to go ahead, *1992*.

Fuck off Norway.

HIS RESPONSE to being asked by a Norwegian TV commentator whether he had a 'message for Norway' before World Cup qualifying match, *1992*.

The doctor at Lazio told me I should try drinking wine because it would be good for me. When I did he took one look at me and said 'you'd better go back on the beer.'

ANSWERING Graham Taylor's suggestion that he drank too much beer, *1993*.

I'm no poof, that's for sure.

REASSURING Terry Wogan, *1990*.

CHAPTER 7

The Middle Men

REFEREES

The lad was sent off for foul and abusive language but he swears blind he didn't say a word.

JOE ROYLE, Oldham manager, on Paul Warhurst's dismissal at Notts County, *1990*.

It takes some believing for a referee to mix up two players as different in appearance as we are. I'm 5 ft 8 in and white, he's 6 ft 4 in and black.

TONY SPEARING, Plymouth defender, after referee booked him and not Tony Witter, the real offender, *1992*.

Thank God they [the referee and his linesmen] are all out there together otherwise they could have spoiled three matches instead of one.

TOMMY DOCHERTY, radio pundit and former manager, at Old Trafford, *1992*.

The referee is available for Christmas pantomime or cabaret.

KEITH VALLE, Tannoy announcer, as Bristol Rovers and Wigan players left the pitch, *1989*. He thought 'the microphone was switched off'.

I thanked the referee for giving us three cracking throw-ins, even when one of them might have been their ball.

NEIL WARNOCK, Notts County manager, during long losing run, *1992*.

Four very strange decisions by the referee totally changed the whole course of the game.

GRAEME SOUNESS, Liverpool manager, after 5–1 defeat at Coventry, *1992*.

You can't even talk to referees now. You go into their room and they tell you to go away. You ask them a question and they won't talk to you.

KENNY DALGLISH, Blackburn manager, *1992*.

I can't really comment – if I said what I wanted to about the referee they would lock me up and throw away the key.

GREG DOWNS, Hereford player-manager, after being one of four Hereford players sent off at Northampton, *1992*.

I'm 27 years old and the referee tells me I'm not allowed to swear.

> VINNIE JONES, Wimbledon midfielder, after being sent off for 'foul and abusive language', *1992.*

You could say it was a penalty but if you look at the other end we should have had three penalties. I've always said that the three boys in black are the three blind mice and it showed today.

> BRUCE GROBBELAAR, Liverpool goalkeeper, after match v Wimbledon, *1992.*

I will swear on my daughters' heads that the referee was badly disposed to me throughout the game.

> DIEGO MARADONA, after being sent off playing for Seville, *1993.*

He should go back to concentrating on medicine and not carry on causing damage to soccer.

> CARLOS MENEM, President of Argentina, on the World Cup final referee, Edgardo Codesal Mendez, a gynaecologist, *1990.*

We don't referee to win popularity contests.

> ROGER WISEMAN, asking the Football League to be removed from their panel after being assaulted by pitch-invading fans during Birmingham v Stoke match, *1992.*

I hope it doesn't sound conceited or arrogant, but the top referees make very few mistakes. I'm like a salesman – I'm selling decisions to players and I think I've been a reasonably successful salesman . . . .I feel I'm the conductor of the orchestra and the orchestra doesn't play as well without a skilled conductor.

> GEORGE COURTNEY, shortly before retiring, *1992.*

I'd like to see them become policemen on traffic duty rather than conductors in an orchestra.

> GORDON TAYLOR, Professional Footballers' Association chief executive, *1991.*

We are stage managers not performers.

> ALAN GUNN, FA Cup Final referee, *1990.*

I do it because I was a useless player.

> JIM RUSHTON, Football League referee, *1991.*

Jim would be devastated without football in his life.

> ISABEL RUSHTON, Jim's wife.

'Gary Lineker's just shaken hands with Jürgen Klinsmann – it's a wonder he hasn't fallen down.' Ron Atkinson on Klinsmann, seen above in characteristic action

'Someone asked me if I missed the Villa – I said "No, I live in one".' David Platt (BELOW) on his new life in Italy

'I'd like to retire with half of what he's achieved and a quarter of his dough.'
Dave Bassett on Brian Clough, pictured above before his final game at Forest

'Jack Charlton is not always right but he is never wrong.' Johnny Giles on his
old Leeds colleague and successor as Ireland manager

'Roy Keane doesn't know where his talent comes from. Nobody does – it's just there.' Brian Clough on the former Cobh Rambler (ABOVE LEFT)

'I hate watching – it's making me go grey.' Peter Reid (ABOVE RIGHT) on his preference for the first part of the player-manager's role

'Comparing Gascoigne with the Phantom of the Opera is to do the Phantom an injustice – he's playing more like Sarah Brightman.' Marcus Berkmann, journalist

'What character, what stature, what a patriot, what a player!' Bobby Robson on Terry Butcher (ABOVE LEFT after giving blood for England)

'David Icke (ABOVE RIGHT) says he's here to save the world, but he saved bugger all when he played in goal for Coventry.' Jasper Carrott

'Millions of Americans have been growing grass indoors for years, but they don't usually play football on it.' Scott LeTellier, of World Cup US '94, on staging matches in the covered Pontiac Silverdome (BELOW)

I remember once I reffed Nottingham Forest v Southampton and I cautioned seven and sent one off, and the *Sunday Times* man said he didn't have to look in the programme to know the referee was a headmaster. I've still got that cutting.

GEORGE COURTNEY, *1986*.

There is no place for public criticism of referees.

FRANK CLARK, chief executive of the League Managers' Association, *1993*.

I know what it feels like when it is apparent that at least one incorrect referee's decision has ruined a week's hard work. I can recommend a formula to combat the excruciating pressure and temptation to be spiteful. It is to become a parrot and answer all searching questions on the subject with 'I never discuss referees' decisions after games.'

JIMMY HILL, Fulham chairman and former Coventry manager, *1993*.

I'll have to stop that, I don't think Italian referees appreciate being patted on the head or the bum.

PAUL GASCOIGNE, early in his Lazio career, *1992*.

The referee must have felt like the President of the United States at the time of the Cuban missile crisis.

HOWARD WILKINSON, Leeds manager, after postponement of crunch game v Manchester United because of waterlogged pitch, *1992*.

The laws make no provision for dealing with written dissent from a Prime Minister.

LE QUOTIDIEN DE PARIS, responding to French Premier Michel Rocard's protest about Benfica's 'handball' goal which knocked Marseille out of the European Cup, *1990*.

I never comment on referees and I'm not going to break the habit of a lifetime for that prat.

RON ATKINSON, West Brom manager, after UEFA Cup defeat by Red Star Belgrade, 1979.

AGENTS

Don't know much about the game, don't even like it much. What's that got to do with it? My business is selling people. Makes no difference what they do.

ERIC 'MONSTER' HALL, agent, *1990*.

I wouldn't cross the road to talk to an agent, let alone go to Manchester.

> GRAHAM KELLY, FA chief executive, declining invitation to a meeting attended by agents, *1992*.

We have to deal with these people, but Bill Shankly wouldn't have done.

> BRIAN CLOUGH, *1991*.

I'm talking to you, not your bimbo.

> BRIAN CLOUGH to agent Jon Holmes during transfer discussions with Leicester's Gary McAllister, *1990*.

It's transfers where the agent gets a bad name. The bad agent will put his player into the club, get a percentage of the signing-on fee – some even take a percentage of his salary – get paid by the club for doing the deal – leave him in there for a year – then agitate to get him out, and put him in somewhere else.

> JON SMITH, agent, in Pete Davies, *All Played Out: The Full Story of Italia '90, 1990*.

I realised just how sinister it had become when I was manager of Peterborough and tried to sign a lad who had played only one League game. He told me to talk to his agent. There are 2000 professional footballers in England, but only about 20 of them need an agent.

> MARK LAWRENSON, former Peterborough manager and Republic of Ireland defender, on his work as an alternative 'agent', backed by the players' union, *1991*.

Every player needs an agent because whatever their status in the game they are in no position to negotiate their own contracts. As for signing up the young players I see nothing wrong in that. I also handle showbiz people and often take on groups before they've made a record.

> ERIC 'MONSTER' HALL, responding to Lawrenson, *1991*.

CHAPTER 8

This Supporting Life

Miserable specimens . . . learning to be hysterical as they groan or cheer in panic unison with their neighbours, the worst sound of all being the hysterical scream of laughter that greets any trip or fall by a player.

LORD BADEN-POWELL, founder of the Boy Scouts, on football spectators in *Scouting for Boys, 1908.*

Football crowds are never going to sound like the hat parade on the club lawns of Cheltenham Racecourse. They are always going to have more vinegar than Chanel.

ARTHUR HOPCRAFT, author, *The Football Man, 1968.*

English fans are brilliant. In England when you ask someone which club he supports, it means something. The guy supports a club for the whole of his life, whatever the ups and downs. In France, there's no loyalty. If you're not top of the League, the fans go to another club.

ERIC CANTONA, French striker then with Leeds, on hearing that England fans had rioted in Sweden, *1992.*

The supporters don't matter as far as I'm concerned. They just pay their entrance fee. I don't care whether they come to Barnet or not – we play good football whether they are there or not.

STAN FLASHMAN, Barnet chairman, *1992.*

Support means getting behind the team through thick and thin. Newcastle supporters have, in the last few years, been through thin and thin.

KEVIN KEEGAN, after becoming Newcastle manager, *1992.*

At Newcastle the crowd is worth one and a half goals' start to the home side, but here it's probably minus six.

VIC JOBSON, Southend chairman, *1992.*

No true Hearts fan would wish Hibs to be relegated. It is a pleasant thought that we can play them four times a year and be reasonably sure of, say, half a dozen League points. The worst sort of Hibs supporter is the one who says he wants Hearts to win the League if Hibs can't win it. He is lying in his teeth. He is a hypocrite.

> JOHN FAIRGRIEVE, journalist, author and Heart of Midlothian fan, in *The Boys in Maroon, 1986*.

Buoyed by their first-leg victory, Celtic supporters invaded Liverpool en masse for the second leg. In the afternoon they roamed the city centre in vast, intimidating hordes, bringing the traffic to a halt in Church Street while some of their number bowed low in obeisance of a green and white bus.

> IVAN PONTING, author, in Steve Hale and Ivan Ponting, *Liverpool in Europe, 1992*.

I knew my days were numbered when I was warming up behind the goal at Parkhead one day and one of our fans shouted: 'Kinnaird, we like the Poll Tax more than we like you.'

> PAUL KINNAIRD, Partick Thistle player, on his spell with St Mirren, *1992*.

In Glasgow half the football fans hate you and the other half think they own you.

> TOMMY BURNS, Celtic midfielder, *1987*.

I think the BBC should be banned from Ibrox. During the Dunfermline game the cameras showed me sitting in the Copland Stand while I was off work and on the sick. Gies a job.

> LETTER to Rangers fanzine *Follow, Follow, 1990*.

[Fanzines are] a case of successful cultural contestation in and through sport.

> JOHN HORNE, lecturer at Staffordshire Polytechnic and co-author of paper on fanzines in *Sociology Review, 1991*.

The Football Pink

> GAY & LESBIAN football supporters' fanzine title, *1990s*.

It's Half Past Four and We're 2–0 Down

> DUNDEE fanzine title, *1990s*.

Proper Shaped Balls

> CARDIFF CITY fanzine title, *1990s*.

The kind of commitment Scots invest in football means there's less left for the more important concerns.

WILLIAM MCILVANNEY, novelist and journalist, from 13-year-old feature on Scottish independence reprinted in *Surviving the Shipwreck, 1992.*

More Dead Wood than the Mary Rose

PORTSMOUTH fanzine title, *1990s*.

Rebels Without a Clue

SLOUGH TOWN (nickname 'The Rebels') fanzine title, *1980s*.

One Man and His Dog

SCOTTISH junior football fanzine title, *1992*.

The Lad Done Brilliant

FANZINE title, *1990s*.

Look Back in Amber

HULL CITY fanzine title, *1990s*.

Dial M for Merthyr

MERTHYR TYDFIL fanzine, *1990s*.

Never Say Dai

NEWPORT AFC fanzine title, *1990s*.

Hyde! Hyde! What's the Score?

PRESTON fanzine *1990s*. Title refers to North End's 26–0 win v Hyde in 1887.

Loadsamoney

BLACKBURN ROVERS fanzine title, *1990s*.

Born Kicking

WOMEN'S football fanzine title, *1990s*.

Two overused facts: It is every schoolboy's dream to play for Manchester United; West Ham play attractive football.

JUST ANOTHER WEDNESDAY, Sheffield Wednesday fanzine, *1990*.

Three days after joining Partick Thistle, Frank McAvennie says he is 'homesick for London' and joins Barnet . . . . Marseille pay £7 million for Vinnie Jones . . . . West Ham are acclaimed the most entertaining team ever to finish 29 points adrift at the bottom of the Second Division.

BLOW FOOTBALL fanzine's preview of the season, *1989*.

You wouldn't get this [a Nigel Kennedy mini-concert] at a Blues' [Birmingham City] shareholders' meeting.

> DOUG ELLIS, Aston Villa chairman, after the violinist and Villa fan had entertained the club's AGM, *1990*.

Get your Villa fanzine . . . guaranteed not one word on Nigel Kennedy.

> *HEROES & VILLAINS* seller, Villa Park, *1990*.

Same old story. Lost 5–0. Sometimes I wonder why I couldn't have been born in Liverpool.

> RICHARD O. SMITH, editor, in Boston United fanzine *Behind Your Fences*, recalling away trip to Cheltenham, *1990*.

The worse the team, the better the fanzine.

> JOHN HORNE, Staffordshire Polytechnic lecturer and co-author of paper on fanzines in *Sociology Review, 1991*.

We're playing well, but they want goals too!

> ALLY MCCOIST, Scotland striker, on being serenaded by 'Give us a goal' on visit to fans' camp site in Sweden, *1992*.

Man offers marriage proposal to any woman with ticket for Leeds United v Sheffield United game. Must send photograph (of ticket).

> ADVERT in the *Yorkshire Evening Post* as the Second Division championship race hotted up, *1990*.

I have measured out my life in Arsenal fixtures, and any event of any significance has a footballing shadow. When did my first real love affair end? The day after a disappointing 2–2 draw at home to Coventry.

> NICK HORNBY, author, *Fever Pitch: A Fan's Life, 1992*.

I'm certified. I've brought my certificate with me.

> IAN SELF, Plymouth Argyle fan, explaining to the *Daily Telegraph* why he had made the 750-mile round trip to Cambridge on Boxing Day, *1991*.

In Latin countries the supporter wants his team to win in injury time, in an offside position, with a handball, because he can make fun of the other team. He wants the most irregular happening possible.

> JOSE ROBERTO WRIGHT, Brazilian World Cup referee, *1991*.

Match attendance bears some of the marks of churchgoing. Maybe a few are there who couldn't face the inevitable row if they announced to a distraught parent that they no longer wanted to go. ('I've grown out of it, Dad.') Some recall a sudden conversion experience. Football offers both popular devotions for the simple faithful – chanting and arm-waving at matches, holy pictures to display around the home – and the learned scrutiny of tactics and sacred texts for the brahmins and sophisticates.

> BRENDAN WALSH, columnist, *Catholic Herald, 1993*.

Normally we are in bed by 10.30, but we've been given special dispensation to stay up during the World Cup finals.

> FRANCISCAN MONK, Cagliari, *1990*.

It was a bit hard to jump up and down with the chains on.

> BRIAN KEENAN, Irish hostage in Lebanon, on watching Ireland v England World Cup match, in captivity, *1990*.

Sir – Instead of the present 90 minutes (two hours if extra time is played), would it not be possible to decide the outcome of each World Cup match by the penalty shoot-out method? This would result in the whole event being completed in less than a day instead of the interminable month or so that it takes now. It would also ensure that my husband could do something more useful than lying sprawled out on the settee, can of beer in hand, watching the tedious stuff.

> LETTER to *Daily Telegraph* after World Cup finals, *1990*.

He's got very broad musical taste, anything from Elgar and Bach to Genesis and Supertramp. He also supports Arsenal, but then nobody's perfect.

> BRIAN PEARSON, secretary to the Archbishop of Canterbury, Dr George Carey, *1990*.

I am a human being. I support Aston Villa, but I am still a human being.

> JOHN TAYLOR, prospective Conservative candidate for Cheltenham, on being labelled a 'bloody nigger' by Tory opponents, *1990*.

If you removed every adulterer from Parliament, there'd be nobody left, but if I found out a person was a closet Manchester United supporter I would have to think very hard about voting for them.

> ADRIAN HENRI, poet, painter and Liverpool fan, during General Election campaign, *1992*.

Q: What's your idea of perfect happiness?
A: West Ham beating Arsenal 20–0.

> LESLIE GRANTHAM, aka 'Dirty Den' from *EastEnders*, interviewed in *1991*.

Anyone who's had to support the Labour Party these past five years knows what it's like being a West Ham supporter. There's a great similarity in the 'oh, f——g hell', head-in-hands response you have to what they do, the own goals and the ridiculous defeats.

> BILLY BRAGG, pop singer and socialist, *1991*.

If I ever have to leave this club I like to think I'd come back and support them, because I love to watch games at Upton Park, and always will. I'll never stop being a West Ham supporter.

BILLY BONDS, West Ham manager and ex-player, *1991*.

I love my golf and it's a great way to make a living, but if I had to choose between a social round of golf and watching Spurs, football would win every time. If they get to Wembley, you won't see me at the Italian Open.

RUSSELL CLAYDON, European tour golfer, *1991*.

Did you know that the Chancellor, John Major, is a Chelsea fan? And you were wondering why the economy is in such a mess.

YORKSHIRE EVENING POST sports diary, *1990*.

I watched Chelsea long before I got into politics and I shall be watching them long after I have left.

JOHN MAJOR, then Chancellor of the Exchequer, 1990.

Castro called the win by the Cuban volleyball team over the US 'a sporting, psy-chological, patriotic and revolutionary victory'. At Stamford Bridge, we're quite happy to settle for three points.

SEBASTIAN COE, Sports Council official, former athlete and Chelsea fan, *1990*.

I'd never been anywhere except for Wexford and Kerry. I'd never been inside a soc-cer stadium. I hadn't even walked past one. But I had a Chelsea scarf. My mother had knitted it for me. The blue wasn't quite right but it didn't matter; it was a Chelsea scarf, the only one in Kilbarrack. Someone in the school yard tried to pull it off me. It scorched the back of my neck. The skin was crispy back there for days. All for Chelsea.

RODDY DOYLE, novelist and screen-writer, on his boyhood devotion, *1992*.

David Mellor left his Westminster office as Minister of Fun dressed in his business suit.

But underneath he had on the Chelsea football strip he wore for sex sessions with Antonia de Sancha.

Speaking for the first time about her affair with Mellor, the actress told a friend the minister appeared from the bathroom of their lovenest in his favourite team's blue and white kit.

The friend said the 31-year-old Antonia told her he wore a peaked cap carrying the Chelsea logo and the team socks.

Only the shorts were missing.

TODAY newspaper, front-page lead story, *1992*.

Just before five o' clock on Saturday, 6 May 1978 I was sitting five rows behind the Royal Box at Wembley with my dad. He'd taken me to watch Ipswich Town since I was five. We beat Arsenal 1–0 in the FA Cup Final. When the final whistle blew the two of us just sobbed and sobbed. I've never been so happy in my life.

TREVOR NUNN, former Royal Shakespeare Company director, *1992*.

Five Newport County supporters were arrested after they turned up at a Kidderminster Harriers game in drag. About 150 visiting fans arrived in the town but 40 went to the Oxfam shop and bought women's clothes. 'I don't know whether this is a new style or what it is,' said Superintendent Peter Picken.

WORCESTER EVENING NEWS, 1989.

You can't force people to sit down even if they have a seat. They want to sing and unless you're Val Doonican, you can't do that sitting down.

KEVIN KEEGAN, Newcastle manager, speaking against all-seated stadia, *1992*.

Has Macari got a bet?

OLDHAM fans' song during 6–0 win over West Ham, whose manager Lou Macari had allegedly bet against his own team when managing Swindon, *1989*.

Oh lucky, lucky,
Lucky, lucky, lucky Liverpool

CRYSTAL PALACE fans after 9–0 defeat at Liverpool, *1989*.

We all agree, Des Walker is worth more than Derby.

NOTTINGHAM FOREST fans' song at time of proposed sale of neighbouring Derby, *1990*.

Are you Maxwell in disguise?

DERBY fans to referee, *1991*.

We all came in the same taxi.

WIMBLEDON fans' chant at the smallest-ever First Division attendance, *1991*.

You're going home in a military ambulance.

SWINDON fans taunt to Bolton supporters during ambulancemen's dispute, *1989*.

We'll win again, don't know where, don't know when . . . .

SHEFFIELD UNITED fans' song during long barren run, *1990*.

Oleg, Oleg, gies a wave.

RANGERS crowd to uncomprehending new Ukrainian signing, Oleg Kuznetsov, *1990*.

Dicks out! Dicks out!

FULHAM fans' chant, *1991*. Alan Dicks was manager of a struggling Fulham side.

There's only one Bill Wyman.

WEST HAM fans to Pat van den Hauwe, of Spurs, then dating the Rolling Stone's estranged wife Mandy, *1991*.

Don't you think we've had enough?

BIRMINGHAM fans' song, to tune of 'We'll Support You Ever More', during 3–0 home defeat by Cambridge, *1991*.

We're not famous any more.

BIRMINGHAM fans, as above.

What the fuck is going on?

LEEDS fans' song when Liverpool went 4–0 up in 25 minutes at Elland Road, *1991*. Liverpool won 5–4.

Are you watching, Hartlepool?

DARLINGTON fans celebrating the win at Welling which ensured their return to the Football League, *1990*.

We're so broke it's unbelievable.

TOTTENHAM fans' chant at FA Cup Final, Wembley, *1991*.

We all agree, Emmerdale is better than Brookside.

HALIFAX fans' song during FA Cup tie at Marine, on Merseyside, *1992*.

Until South Yorkshire Police go on the record and accept the interim Taylor Report, they are not fit to take charge of more than 40,000 lives.

TREVOR HICKS, Hillsborough Family Support Group chairman, on the FA decision to play another semi-final at Hillsborough, *1992*.

It's an emotive issue. We took that on board by not contemplating a semi-final there involving Liverpool or Nottingham Forest had they got through.

DAVID BLOOMFIELD, FA press officer, responding to Hicks.

There have always been hooligans. In Germany they were in the Gestapo and in Russia they were in the KGB. To treat us unfairly as a club is to become like them, because their justice is rough justice.

HOWARD WILKINSON, Leeds manager, on calls for his club to be punished for their fans' riot at Bournemouth, *1990*.

139

I hope I don't hear anyone saying how glad they are to have won it for such great fans, because that would be sick.

HARRY REDKNAPP, Bournemouth manager, after the Leeds riot.

I believe there is a connection between what happened at Bournemouth [the riot by Leeds fans] and the fact that Leeds is the least hip city in Britain.

TONY WILSON, Manchester-based owner of Factory Records, *1990*.

We have once again had an opportunity to prove that beer and fans don't mix.

DAVID MELLOR MP, Heritage Secretary, after rioting by England fans in Sweden, *1992*.

I thought that the problem with the English hooligans was over but now I know it is not.

LENNART JOHANSSON, president of UEFA, after trouble involving England fans during European Championship finals, *1992*.

If the Prime Minister was to persevere with a policy of hunting down and punishing by whatever means those who disgrace this nation overseas, he might even force a draw in a safe Labour seat. Surely it's time to end tongue-clicking and decent people's frustration and let retribution begin.

JIMMY HILL, former player, manager, TV analyst and Fulham chairman, in *Daily Telegraph* article condemning rioting English fans at European Championship finals, *1992*.

Every British male, at some time or other, goes to his last football match. It may very well be his first football match.

MARTIN AMIS, novelist, reviewing book on 'football' hooliganism, *1991*.

The fans all had the complexion and body-scent of a cheese-and-onion crisp, and the eyes of pit-bulls.

AMIS, recalling his experience of watching Queen's Park Rangers, *1991*.

Casting football supporters as 'belching subhumanity' makes it easier for us to be treated as such, and therefore easier for tragedies like Hillsborough to occur. Writers are welcome at football – the game does not have the literature it deserves. But snobs slumming it with 'the lads' – there is nothing we need less.

ED HORTON, Oxford fan, responding to Amis and the author of the book he reviewed, Bill Buford, in *When Saturday Comes* magazine, *1991*.

All that is needed to stop football hooliganism is that soccer fans should have a good catharsis before and after every game – shout, scream, talk gibberish – to release all pent-up violence.

BHAGWAN RAJNEESH, Indian 'sex guru', *1989*.

You thought there was hate out there with all the fans spitting – you were here on a good day.

> DAVID KOHLER, Luton chief executive, to journalists on supporters' demonstrations against him, *1993*.

It's not surprising some fans behave badly when it is realised how little consideration they receive from the clubs.

> COLIN SMITH, Chief Constable, Thames Valley Police, *1990*.

Did I get any enjoyment at all from my visit to Marston Road? Well, as a matter of fact, I did. Guessing the contents of the liquid which came out of the tea urn fired my imagination for some time.

> LETTER by Stafford Rangers fan to *Staffordshire Newsletter*, 1992.

Six soccer hooligans were brought back to court yesterday and rewarded with their freedom for going to the help of prison officers during a break-out . . . . The Stoke City fans, aged between 17 and 20, from Alsager, Cheshire, were freed by Judge Robin David QC at Knutsford Crown Court for refusing to take part in an escape on Friday at Sale.

> *DAILY TELEGRAPH* report, *1991*.

I heard this bloke in the stand shouting 'McGraw [Alan, manager], we're f——g sick of what you're doing to Morton, buying bastards like Gahagan.' Two minutes later I scored the winner and as I was running back I heard this same guy shouting, 'Yes Johnny boy, gies another one!'

> JOHN GAHAGAN, Morton player, *1990*.

Joey ate the Frogs' legs
Made the Swiss roll
Now he's Munching Gladbach

> LIVERPOOL fans' banner in praise of defender Joey Jones, European Cup Final, Rome, *1977*.

The Darling Buds of Eddie May

> CARDIFF fans' banner, *1993*. May was coach as the club won promotion.

Europe – Scouse-free Zone

> MANCHESTER UNITED fans' T-shirt slogan as their club returned to continental competition while Liverpool remained banned, *1990*.

Mel's Marvels 5 Fergie's Wallet 1

> MANCHESTER CITY fans' T-shirt slogan after 'derby' victory by Mel Machin's side, *1989*.

Italy – Land of no Poll Tax

> SCOTTISH banner at World Cup finals, *1990*.

Anneka Rice – A Challenge – Get a Drink in Genoa

> SCOTTISH fans' banner during 'dry' World Cup finals, *1990*.

Even Our Cat Hates Howard Kendall

> MANCHESTER CITY fans' banner after Kendall returned to Everton from Maine Road, *1991*.

Kendall robbed Derek and Mavis

> CITY fans' banner at match, at time of a 'mystery theft' in *Coronation Street, 1990*.

Theo's Cobblers Squash Creepy Crawley

> NORTHAMPTON fans' banner at FA Cup tie v Crawley Town, *1991*.Theo Foley's team lost 4–2.

The Silence of the Rams

> SLOGAN on anti-Derby T-shirt sold outside Nottingham Forest's ground, *1993*.

We want T, No Sugar

> SLOGAN on fan's placard at Tottenham during feud between Terry Venables and Alan Sugar, *1993*.

England expects you to kill Spicks, Dagoes, Commies and Frogs.

> SLOGAN on World Cup T-shirt on sale in Blackpool, *1990*.

Visiting supporters will be kept behind for 10 minutes after the final whistle to allow the ground to clear . . . and the Wrexham fans will be kept in until Saturday's match with Blackpool.

> TANNOY announcer at Wrexham to 18,000 crowd at FA Cup replay v West Ham, *1992*.

'Give me,' Mick was saying, 'the four men that've played for Scotland an' their names've only got three letters in them.'

Frankie hoped for the stranger's sake that he didn't get it right. Doing well in one of Mick's casual football quizzes was a doubtful honour, earning you the right to face more and more obscure questions the relevance to which of football wasn't easy to see. 'Tell me,' Frankie had once said to Mick by way of parody, 'in what Scotland–England game did it rain for four-and-a-half minutes at half-time? And how wet was the rain?'

> WILLIAM MCILVANNEY in the short story 'Performance' from the collection *Walking Wounded, 1989*.

CHAPTER 9

A Woman's Place

Women should be in the kitchen, the discotheque and the boutique but not in football.

> RON ATKINSON, Sheffield Wednesday manager, *1989*.

I've always believed in treating the ball like a woman. Give it a cuddle, caress it a wee bit, take your time, and you'll get the required response.

> JIM BAXTER, Rangers and Scotland player of the 1960s, *1991*.

Why not treat the wife to a weekend in London and let her go shopping on Saturday afternoon while you go and watch the Latics play West Ham?

> OLDHAM programme, *1991*.

It's a bloody stupid colour. I think one of the directors' wives must have chosen it.

> DAVID PLEAT, Luton manager, announcing the end of his club's 'unlucky' tangerine away kit, *1992*.

They are nice people with a part to play but at the end of the day they are tea-ladies who do not understand the game.

> TREVOR STEELE, resigning as chairman of Bradford Park Avenue in the Bass North West Counties League after two women directors were elected to the board, *1990*.

The FA have had enough money off me this season. Mrs Gould won't let me give them any more fines.

> BOBBY GOULD, Coventry manager, refusing to comment on a sending-off, *1993*.

Women run everything. The only thing I've done within my house in the last 20 years is recognise Angola as an independent state.

> BRIAN CLOUGH, Nottingham Forest manager, *1992*.

As long as people like this are running football, the game will be governed by prejudice and stereotypes. Haven't they watched *The Manageress* on television?

> FIONA FOX, Equal Opportunities Commission spokesperson, on Leicester City's advertisement for a male press officer, *1990*.

Our last Prime Minister was a woman. The head of the Royal Family is a woman. And the head of Birmingham City is a woman.

KARREN BRADY, Birmingham managing director, explaining why she believed men and women 'received equal treatment in society', *1993.*

144

We don't feel it would be suitable for a female to be put with a dozen naked footballers as they get ready to jump into the bath. Apart from anything else, the language used is sometimes very industrial.

> PETER HILL, Leicester commercial manager, answering Ms Fox, *1990*.

I married a girl who was very easily told: 'If you marry me you're marrying football.'

> GRAHAM TAYLOR, England manager, *1992*.

The real reason I'm back? The wife just wants me out of the house.

> KENNY DALGLISH on returning to management with Blackburn, *1991*.

My idea of relaxation: Going somewhere away from the wife.

> TERRY FENWICK, QPR captain, in *Match* magazine, *1986*.

When I said even my Missus could save us from relegation, I was exaggerating.

> PETER TAYLOR, Derby manager, *1982*.

THE MRS MADE ME DO IT

> *SUN* headline on Ron Atkinson's defection from Sheffield Wednesday to Aston Villa, *1991*. Atkinson derided reports that he had been 'hen-pecked' into the move.

Most Dangerous Opponent: My ex-wife.

> FRANK WORTHINGTON, in answer to magazine questionnaire, *1982*.

My wife says it would be better if there was another woman. At least then she'd know what she was up against. But she says, 'How can I compete with a football?'

> DON MACKAY, Blackburn Rovers manager, *1988*.

Just ask my wife what this club means to me. She says I'm married to it.

> DOUG ELLIS, Aston Villa chairman, *1990*.

Leaving a club is like leaving a woman. When you have nothing left to say, you go.

> ERIC CANTONA, Manchester United striker, after leaving Leeds, *1992*.

Get back in there and tell him you've had enough and want to go.

> JANE VARADI to husband Imre after match in which he was substituted by Sheffield Wednesday manager Peter Eustace, *1989*.

The court said it was unusual for a husband to complain about his wife spending too much time on football.

> WENDY TOMS, the first woman referee to make the Football League's reserve list, on her divorce, *1991*.

Having a Football League club is like having a good wife – you only appreciate it when it's lost.

> JONATHAN CRISP, Colchester chairman, during the club's exile in the Vauxhall Conference, *1991*.

How did I get the black eye? My wife gave it to me.

> DANNY WILSON, Sheffield Wednesday midfielder, *1992*.

If there is already stress and strain in a marriage, watching too much of the World Cup can lead to aggression and arguments, and possibly violence.

> SPOKESWOMAN for Relate, formerly the Marriage Guidance Council, *1990*.

There's this staunch Stoke fan who's getting some pre-match earache from his missus. 'You'd rather go and watch Stoke City than take me out,' she complains. 'Correction,' he replies, 'I'd rather go and watch Port Vale than take you out.'

> PETE CONWAY, Potteries comedian, *1991*.

He looked into my eyes
Just as an airplane roared above
Said something about football
But he never mentioned love.

> KIRSTY MacCOLL, singer, on song co-written with Jem Finer, 'He Never Mentioned Love', *1991*.

I know it sounds awful, but it just hit me half-way through my stag night that I'd rather be going to the match with the lads than marrying Nicola.

> KEVIN MCCALL, Hereford fan, cancelling his wedding to watch Hereford play Aylesbury in the FA Cup, *1991*.

Fewer than one in five Midlanders would miss a match to attend the wedding of his partner's best friend.

> FABERGÉ SURVEY, *1990*.

If there really are men who prefer football to girls, I've never met any.

> SHARON KNIGHT, 19-year-old Miss Stoke-on-Trent, *1990*.

I couldn't compete with her. Andy said he wanted to stay in England and I could see why.

> DAVID HAY, St Mirren manager, after failing to entice Watford's Andy Kennedy north, *1991*. Kennedy's girlfriend was model Maria Whittaker.

Football is rife with rumours. Footballers are the worst gossips – they're worse than women.

> LEE CHAPMAN, Leeds striker, *1992*.

My granny could have swept some of those chances in.

> GERRY FRANCIS, Bristol Rovers manager, *1990*.

It was handbag stuff. If you start sending people off for scratching at each other then you might as well send a team out wearing skirts.

> KENNY HIBBITT, Walsall manager, after one of his players was sent off v Cardiff, *1992*.

My lot are a bunch of fairies who couldn't kick a ball as far as my wife.

> TERRY COOPER, Exeter City manager, after a defeat at Bournemouth, *1991*.

We defended like women.

> JOE ROYLE, Oldham manager, after 5–2 defeat at Wimbledon, *1992*.

I hate football. I think most women do. It's not the sort of sport I'm interested in. I prefer the indoor sort of games.

> CYNTHIA PAYNE, Streatham 'Madam', before the World Cup finals, *1990*.

It appears that the lady in question was the owner of a massage parlour protesting at a decision to tax her earnings . . . . contrary to some suggestions I have received, I did not ask for her phone number; I just advised her to contact her local MP.

> LEE CHAPMAN, Leeds striker, after a female streaker ran on during match at Sheffield Wednesday, *1992*.

I'm so bad at cooking that I phone my girlfriend to send over some food. She cooks it and puts it on a plate, covers it with silver foil and gets a taxi to drive it over.

> JOHN FASHANU, Wimbledon striker, *1991*.

Players don't mess with me now. I've sent two off this season and they have to live with the extra humiliation that they've been sent off by a woman.

> WENDY TOMS, referee, on her promotion to the Football League reserve list, *1991*.

147

The most pressing ambition of many of these girls, which surprised me, was to play football.

> ROS COWARD, *Guardian* journalist, reporting from two London schools on whether girls still wanted to be hairstylists, nurses and ballerinas, *1991*.

We just don't like males and females playing together. I like feminine girls. Anyway, it's not natural.

> TED CROKER, FA chief executive, *1988*.

Women's football is a game that should only be played by consenting adults in private.

> BRIAN GLANVILLE, journalist, *1990*.

I never expected to get the man-of-the-match award.

> LESLEY SHIPP, Arsenal Ladies' player, after Women's FA Cup Final win v Doncaster Belles, *1993*.

Each player would nominate a partner (wife, girlfriend or mother) who would be called on to 'kiss it better' in the event of a player going down as if pole-axed. The subsequent derision would soon end this appalling sham.

> LETTER to *The Observer*, European Championship finals, *1992*.

A feminist colleague of mine literally refused to believe that I watched Arsenal, a disbelief that apparently had its roots in the fact that we had once had a conversation about a feminist novel. How could I have possibly read the book *and* have been to Highbury? Tell a thinking woman that you like football and you're in for a pretty sobering glimpse of the female conception of the male.

> NICK HORNBY, author and former teacher, in *Fever Pitch: A Fan's Life, 1992*.

Sarah Michelle Sue Sarah Sandra Sandra Sandra Wendy Heather Rita Karen Susan Denise Shelly Julie Rachel Julie Maxine Bridger.

> BIRTH CERTIFICATE entry for Midlands baby born during World Cup finals, and named after wives and girlfriends of England squad, *1990*.

If a woman suggested the simplest way of brightening up football was by making the goal a bit bigger, they'd say she didn't understand the game and why didn't she go off and practise her netball.

> NIGELLA LAWSON, columnist, *Evening Standard*, on FIFA president Joao Havelange's suggestion to widen the goals, *1990*.

Doing well in football is like childbirth – it doesn't happen overnight.

> BRIAN CLOUGH, Nottingham Forest manager, *1991*.

I like a challenge. If I had been a woman I would have been pregnant all the time because I cannot say no.

> ROBERT MAXWELL, Derby chairman, on his interest in 'saving' Spurs, *1990*.

Like a woman, I might exercise my prerogative to change my mind.

> BRIAN CLOUGH, on retiring as Forest manager, *1993*.

I'm a young, single woman and what I do with my spare time is pretty irrelevant as long as I don't bring the game into disrepute.

> KARREN BRADY, managing director, Birmingham City, *1993*.

— CHAPTER 10 —

Headline Views

PRESS

No comment gentlemen, sorry. You just make it all up anyway.

> STEVE COPPELL, Crystal Palace manager, to reporters at Sheffield United, *1991*.

I don't want to say anything – not even 'no comment'.

> RON ATKINSON, Aston Villa manager, questioned about his interest in Dean Saunders, *1992*.

I've learned with age. I was caught out when I was young, not realising what the tabloids are like. Now I never answer yes or no to any question. They'll ask you, for example, are you going to beat Italy and if you say yes, the headline is: 'We'll beat the Italians!'

> GARY LINEKER, *1992*.

My little daughter could write what they write.

> CHRIS WADDLE, England midfielder, as press–squad relations soured at World Cup finals, *1990*.

Mistrust of the press is a standard feature of any English international footballer.

> PETE DAVIES, author, *All Played Out: The Full Story of Italia '90, 1990*.

I think you'll find it's quite obvious the players think the British press is not with the team.

> BOBBY ROBSON, England manager, at World Cup finals, *1990*.

A very nice bunch of bastards.

> GRAHAM TAYLOR, England manager, describing the accompanying press pack in Norway, *1993*.

[Journalists] are verbal terrorists.

> JESUS GIL, Atletico Madrid president, *1992*.

The glory of the sports pages is but the worship of false idols and tempts him not.

> BILLY BRAGG, singer-songwriter, in song 'God's Footballer' about Peter Knowles, former Wolves striker and Jehovah's Witness, *1991*.

As it was the media who had tipped us to win, I thought one or two of their jobs might be in jeopardy. Not likely. It was me they were after.

BOBBY ROBSON, former England manager, referring to failure in the 1988 European Championships in *Against All Odds, 1990.*

Shame fills the heart of every right-thinking Englishman. How could our lads play like that? How could they let us down so badly?

SUN leader column after England's opening game, a draw v Ireland, World Cup, *1990.*

They couldn't play, sneered the critics. They couldn't string two passes together. How wrong the world was.

SUN leader column after England's semi-final exit v Germany.

During Scotland's 1974 World Cup in Frankfurt, my English colleagues – remember 'Britain' didn't qualify for that one – labelled us 'fans with typewriters'. Here's an update: the English Brat Pack are hooligans with computers.

JIM BLAIR, columnist in Scotland's *Daily Record*, on press attacks on England manager Graham Taylor, *1992.*

Here I am, tear me limb from limb.

GORDON McKEAG, Newcastle chairman, to reporters after relegation, *1989.*

If a journalist watches a game and says 'I thought the lad was crap today', and writes 'He is crap', I'm quite happy with that. But it's trying to put words into people's mouths and making things up that aren't really there – that's what I don't enjoy.

STUART PEARCE, Nottingham Forest captain, explaining his reluctance to talk to the press, *1991.*

Our lot [at Forest] can talk to the press seven days a week for all I care. But in the end experience tells them – and me – to say nowt.

BRIAN CLOUGH, *1990.*

'Blind, Disabled, Press'

SIGN above ticket-collection window at Leeds, *1991.*

I cover Everton matches too, but if war was declared I think I know which side I'd be on.

TOMMY SMITH, ex-Liverpool captain, on his new role as a journalist, *1991.*

Reporter: In my piece on David Platt possibly going to an Italian club I used the word Machiavellian. Would you check the spelling for me?

Sub-editor: How do I do that? Is he the president of Bari or something?

> EXCHANGE at *Birmingham Post, 1991*.

The most exciting moment of the game was when Taddy Smith's powerful drive sailed out of the ground and straight through the window of a nearby house.

> *WHITBY GAZETTE* report on Whitby Town v Whickham, Northern League match, *1992*.

[Since Hartlepool last scored] you could have watched all three *Godfather* movies, waded through *every* technicolour moment of *Gone With the Wind*, and still had time to settle down to a two-hour episode of *Inspector Morse*.

> *HARTLEPOOL MAIL* on the club's record-breaking run without a goal, *1993*.

You haven't come up here to do all that 'dark, satanic mills' stuff, have you, because we've heard it all before.

> YORKSHIRE journalist to London-based reporter, Halifax press box, *1983*.

I don't want to read any of that 'plucky wee Bankies' shite. We had our chance and we blew it.

> JIM FALLON, Clydebank coach, to press when his team had lost a Scottish Cup tie to Aberdeen after leading, *1993*.

If I have given, however inadvertently, the impression that football writers who go abroad fit in their journalistic obligations between drunken orgies, an apology is necessary. We are, in the main, a responsible body of men who are only too well aware of our good luck. We do fall by the wayside, now and again, but it is not unknown for directors – elderly gents, pillars of the establishment at home – to do likewise, and dramatically. Essentially, we usually get the score right, to say nothing of the scorers' names, and that's not bad.

> JOHN FAIRGRIEVE, journalist and author, in *Away Wi' the Goalie, 1977*.

It's the headline writers back in the office who twist things. I got caught again only yesterday. One tabloid quoted me as saying: 'I'm not standing here saying I'll beat Bobby Charlton's record, only time will tell.' They used those words in the story – but the headline said 'I'll Beat Bobby!' Exactly what I hadn't said. I laughed aloud.

> GARY LINEKER, *1992*.

LOONY ROONS BARGY ARGIES

> *SUN* headline after Cameroon beat Argentina, World Cup finals, *1990*.

Roger Milla 'No' to Saddlers

> *WALSALL OBSERVER* headline on one of the more unlikely transfer bids, *1990*.

I'LL SPILL BEANS ON SWINDON

TODAY headline about allegations of corruption at Swindon Town, *1990*.

United supporter to be next Pope

EVENING CHRONICLE, Newcastle-upon-Tyne, headline on story speculating that Cardinal Basil Hume would be elected to the Vatican, *1980s*.

FROGS DUMP BEARDO

DAILY STAR headline on French clubs' alleged loss of interest in buying Peter Beardsley, *1989*.

SOCCER STAR CUT OFF MY KITTY'S PRIVATES

THE PEOPLE headline on story alleging castration of a cat by a Leeds reserve player, *1989*.

PACKIE HAS THE HANDS OF GOD

IRISH PAPER headline after Pat 'Packie' Bonner's penalty shoot-out save Romania World Cup finals, *1990*.

SWEDES 2 TURNIPS 1

SUN headline after England's defeat by Sweden, *1992*.

I'm beginning to wonder what the bloody national vegetable is in Norway.

GRAHAM TAYLOR, England manager, seen here talking to the press before game in Oslo, after being compared to a turnip and an onion after games v Sweden and Spain, *1992*.

YANKS 2 PLANKS 0

SUN headline after USA's victory over England, *1993*.

NORSE MANURE!

SUN headline after Scotland's 0–0 draw in friendly in Norway, *1992*.

ERIC IDOL!

DAILY MIRROR headline after Eric Cantona's hat-trick for Leeds v Spurs, *1992*.

BAYERN KAPUTT!

BILD headline after Bayern Munich's 6–2 defeat by BK 1903 Copenhagen, *1991*.

CLOUGHIE GRABBED MY GOOLIES

DAILY SPORT headline on story involving allegations by Shrewsbury reserve player, *1989*.

Yanks rate Arsenal as exciting as a slice of cold pizza

EVENING STANDARD headline on League champions' impact at Miami tournament, *1989*.

Starship Spectacular: 47,000 Ballpark Fans See UFO!

NATIONAL ENQUIRER (US) headline, on story alleging sighting of spaceship over Old Trafford, *1992*.

VICINI, WHY?

GAZZETTA DELLO SPORT headline after Italy's exit from World Cup, *1990*. Azeglio Vicini was Italy's World Cup coach.

I never speak, according to the newspapers. I just storm and blast.

KEN BATES, Chelsea chairman, *1990*.

It's important to have women in the press box. There's so much that is patronising in sports coverage, the assumption that you are there for Gary Lineker's legs. I don't think a woman watches a football match any differently from a man and lots of women go to matches. We can do without the condescension and the idea that things have to be explained in words of one syllable.

ELEANOR OLDROYD, Radio 5 sports reporter, *1992*.

One or two poor results and all of a sudden, your reports are edged in black.

ROY HODGSON, English manager of Switzerland, to reporters, *1992*.

You lot got rid of [Neil] Kinnock. You must be able to do something about referees.

BOBBY GOULD, Coventry manager, to assembled journalists after match at Norwich, *1993*.

TELEVISION

I'm going to go from the man who invented Roland Rat to the man who lost football.

> GREG DYKE, chairman of ITV Sport, on his company's failed bid for rights to cover Premier League, *1992*.

The biggest advance in TV football since the invention of the camera.

> DAVID HILL, BSkyB head of sport, on the satellite TV company's £304 million deal with the Premier League, *1992*.

The most ludicrous and backward step football has taken in a long time.

> ALEX FERGUSON, Manchester United manager, on the Sky deal, *1992*.

One old lady phoned to say the fireworks made her cat bolt out of the door and she hasn't seen it since.

> BRIAN TRUSCOTT, Southampton secretary, on BSkyB's pre-game show, *1992*.

Young man, you couldn't ask me a hard question to save your life.

> BRIAN CLOUGH, Nottingham Forest manager, to BSkyB reporter David Livingstone, *1992*.

We are in the first stages of saturation coverage. If I go to a match in Europe, I come back to a stack of videos and I can hardly be bothered to watch them. What's going on in *Coronation Street* is what I want to know.

> GRAHAM TAYLOR, England manager, as Sky's contract began to take effect, *1992*.

People are going to say it is cheaper to watch it on telly as well as to avoid traffic problems. We could get the situation where we have two dozen clubs playing in front of empty houses. Then, if the TV figures fall because of saturation coverage, football will not get the same deal the next time negotiations come round.

> TAYLOR, as above.

The governing body of football: television.

> MIKE INGHAM, football correspondent, BBC Radio Sport, *1991*.

I don't think TV is becoming too powerful. At the end of the day the choice rests with football. The decisions are taken by the people who run our football clubs.

> HOWARD WILKINSON, Leeds manager, on the redrawing of the Premier League programme for BSkyB's schedules, *1992*.

It looks like a night of disappointment for Scotland, brought to you live by ITV in association with National Power.

> BRIAN MOORE, ITV commentator, during Scotland v Brazil match, World Cup finals, *1990*.

Nobody I've ever played with has said 'I'm as sick as a parrot' when I've asked them how they were. But thrust a microphone in front of them, and it all comes out: 'It was a game of two halves', 'We'll take each match as it comes', 'The boy done good'. *We've* caught it from *them* – we're as sick as a commentator.

> GARY LINEKER addressing the Oxford Union in a debate on the motion 'This House believes it is better to commentate than to participate', *1990*.

Those who participate provide the poetry. Those who commentate provide the prose. And not very good prose at that. That's why so many ex-players have taken up commentating. It's called missionary work.

> LINEKER, as above. The former England captain later took up punditry on BBC TV's *Match of the Day*.

I start getting nervous about ten minutes before I go on – start getting the hot flushes. But the pressure is nothing like when I was playing. Then, from 2.15 to 3.00 p.m. on Saturdays was purgatory, ten times worse than this.

> ALAN HANSEN, *Match of the Day* analyst and former Liverpool captain, *1993*.

John Motson: I'm trying to be referee, mathematician and commentator. Now it's your turn, Bobby.
Bobby Charlton: The game is nicely poised, it could go either way.

> EXCHANGE during BBC commentary at World Cup finals, *1990*.

What makes [John Motson's] pronouncements all the more cherishable is the realisation that his more lunatic observations – usually in the form of a poetic attempt to capture the essence of a game – are prepared in advance. His precis of the 1988 Wimbledon v Liverpool match, 'the Crazy Gang have beaten the Culture Club', is for true devotees the pinnacle of the man's art, although the alliterative masterpiece he used to hail the new European champions – 'it's dramatic, it's delightful, it's Denmark' – showed that all the time spent alone with the *Rothman's Football Year Book* had not been in vain.

> ALLAN DAVIDSON, journalist, in article headed 'Talking Balls', *FHM* magazine, *1992*.

I'd read that the number of steps up to the royal box was 39. Nothing in that until I remembered that the Manchester United captain was Martin Buchan, so I wrote down a little phrase: 'And how appropriate that there should be 39 steps for Buchan to climb to receive the Cup'. I had not been satisfied at all by my performance during that game and I think that a number of people who had been watching me were thinking much the same. They were rather impressed when that little ad lib came out at the end. But of course it wasn't an ad lib – I'd written it down.

I promise you, though, it's the only time it has happened.

JOHN MOTSON, BBC TV commentator, recalling the 1977 FA Cup Final, his first, *1992*.

Jimmy Hill is to football what King Herod was to babysitting.

TOMMY DOCHERTY, former football manager, *1992*.

Jimmy Hill knows a lot about goalkeeping, doesn't he? He played at the top for how long?

KENNY DALGLISH, Liverpool manager, answering Hill's blaming Bruce Grobbelaar for Liverpool's FA Cup semi-final defeat, *1990*.

Emlyn Hughes puts on a joke act while Jimmy Greaves, with his brash T-shirts and remarks, comes near to portraying the kind of 'football louts' we're trying to get rid of.

KENNETH WOLSTENHOLME, former BBC TV commentator, on ITV's World Cup coverage, *1990*.

I don't know what's going on out there, but whatever it is it's diabolical.

JIMMY GREAVES, ITV pundit, during League Cup tie, *1991*.

Stuart Pearce has got the taste of Wembley in his nostrils.

JOHN MOTSON, BBC TV commentator, *1991*.

The man who is dangerous is the one on the right wing with the sun-tan lotion, Gheorghe Hagi.

RON ATKINSON, ITV pundit, World Cup finals, *1990*.

Poland nil, England nil, though England are now looking better value for their nil.

BARRY DAVIES, commentating for BBC 1, *1989*.

That ball was glued to his foot – all the way into the back of the net.

ALAN PARRY, ITV commentator, World Cup finals, *1990*.

They've obviously seen a slight kink in the Yugoslavian 'keeper.

RAY WILKINS, BBC pundit, World Cup finals, *1990*.

Mike Channon: We've got to get bodies in the box. The French do it, the Italians do it, the Brazilians do it . . . . .
Brian Clough: Yes, even educated bees do it.

EXCHANGE ON ITV panel, World Cup finals, *1986*.

Hades 3 Hendon O

CEEFAX version of hell-raising result from Diadora League match at Hayes, *1992*.

Viv Anderson has pissed a fatness test.

JOHN HELM, ITV commentator, *1991*.

2–0 is a cricket score in Italian football.

ALAN PARRY, ITV commentator, World Cup finals, *1990*.

And the German stormtroopers are arriving at the far post.

BARRY DAVIES, BBC TV commentator, Germany v CIS, *1992*.

And there's a camera suspended above the pitch – I only hope it's screwed in properly.

ARCHIE MACPHERSON, TV commentator, World Cup finals, *1990*.

CHAPTER 11

Board Games

MOGULS AND MEDIOCRITIES

Beware of the clever sharp men who are creeping into the game.

WILLIAM MCGREGOR, founder of the Football League, in *League Football and the Men Who Made It, 1909*.

Why sleep when you can make money?

STAN FLASHMAN, ticket-broker and Barnet chairman, in build-up to FA Cup Final, *1991*.

I'm not a member of the Salvation Army. Football clubs can be a commercial proposition yielding 10 per cent a year.

ROBERT MAXWELL, then Oxford chairman and millionaire publisher, on his 1984 interest in buying Manchester United in Michael Crick and Tony Smith, *Betrayal of a Legend, 1989*.

I threatened to quit over the sale of Dean Saunders, but Maxwell sacked me. He told me: 'No one resigns on the Maxwells.'

MARK LAWRENSON, former Oxford manager, *1993*.

Robert Maxwell's record in football is exemplary . . . . He has always been a person who is prepared to invest heavily in football at a time when others are turning their backs on the game. Some people seem to doubt him, but they don't know the man.

IRVING SCHOLAR, Tottenham chairman, on Maxwell's attempt to take control, *1990*.

If a supporter asked me about that [lending £1.1 million to Spurs to buy Gary Lineker] I would tell him to get stuffed. What I do with my money is my business. Haven't I already done enough for Derby? They were in the knacker's yard when I was invited to help them.

ROBERT MAXWELL, answering criticism during his time as owner of Derby County, who were operating a transfer 'freeze' at the time, *1990*.

I have shown the yellow card to these boardroom squabbles. It is inconceivable that I would entertain having discussions about a rights issue, or become involved with a club where the board are behaving like little children.

> MAXWELL on the Tottenham board's reaction to his offer, *1990*.

[Robert Maxwell's] sense of humour was evident when he described as 'very good investigative journalism' a report in the *Daily Mirror*. The paper trumpeted 'a £12m plan to make Spurs the new kings of Europe'. Maxwell would become 'England's mega-millionaire soccer baron, equivalent to the game's wealthiest patrons in the world, following in the footsteps of Gianni Agnelli at Juventus, Silvio Berlusconi of Milan and Bernard Tapie of Marseille'. This was another joke. Juventus spent £25 million on players last summer alone. As Manchester United have discovered, £12 million does not even make you kings of Lancashire.

> PATRICK BARCLAY, football correspondent, *The Independent, 1990*.

Maxwell chairman? We may as well have Max Wall.

> *THE SHEEP*, Derby County fanzine, *1990*.

Who can blame the Hibs fans for ripping up their scarves, disgusted by the strange dealings which will send their 115-year-old club to the knacker's yard . . . . It's a bad day for Scotland if big money ends up killing off our clubs.

> *DAILY RECORD* editorial on Hearts chairman Wallace Mercer's takeover bid for Hibernian, *1990*. The *Record* was then owned by Robert Maxwell.

Regretfully Robert Maxwell mirrors one of the unfortunate traits of the modern game. He can afford the price of admission, but he doesn't appreciate the value of decorum.

> ANDY WILLIAMSON, Football League assistant secretary, *1990*.

Football attracts a certain percentage of nobodies who want to be somebodies at a football club.

> BRIAN CLOUGH, Nottingham Forest manager, *1979*.

To these nobody-somebodies, managers are, as they are frequently reminded, just employees. Big Ron is not in *Who's Who*, nor are Cloughie or El Tel, although the publication is stuffed with directors, chairmen and vice-presidents of football clubs.

> MARK LAWSON, journalist, reflecting on Clough's comments, *The Independent Magazine, 1991*.

What do directors think of managers? I walked with Jack Tinn [Portsmouth manager] into a Glasgow lounge bar where Jim Taylor, chairman of Preston, was entertaining friends. 'Managers, ten a penny,' said Taylor. 'Directors, they haven't got a price,' replied Tinn.

> JIMMY GUTHRIE, first players' union chairman, in *Soccer Rebel, 1976*.

160

The club directors, clearly, didn't know if they were coming or going; provoked beyond restraint, they would from time to time erupt, like small postulations of marsh gas.

BRIAN GLANVILLE, author, in novel *The Rise of Gerry Logan, 1963*.

Rule 1: I am always right. Rule 2: When I am wrong, read Rule 1.

SIGN above desk in Jersey office of multi-millionaire Jack Walker, Blackburn's benefactor, *1991*.

Because football is good for society.

DAVID SULLIVAN, *Daily Sport* publisher, on why he had bought controlling interest in Birmingham City, *1993*.

I tried to buy Monaco, but I found out some guy called Rainier had got there first.

KEN BATES, Chelsea chairman, *1989*.

Normal business principles don't apply in football.

LIONEL PICKERING, Derby vice-chairman and owner, after investing £9 million in the club, *1992*.

I'm very self-critical. When I get up in the morning I look in the mirror and tell myself what an idiot I am for all the mistakes I made the previous day.

KEN BATES, Chelsea chairman, *1990*

I'm not difficult to work for if you are good at your job, but I don't suffer fools gladly.

BATES, *1991*.

For a start I'm good at football, not property developing or selling pork sausages, like the other chairmen.

TERRY VENABLES, Tottenham manager, outlining his soon-to-be-fulfilled ambition to own and run a club, in afterword to Fred Venables, *Terry Venables: Son of Fred, 1991*.

I can see now why Terry Venables wants to buy his own club.

DON HOWE after being sacked as QPR manager, *1991*.

One chairman told me his club had only had 23 managers since the war, and I said: 'Why man, the war's only been over four weeks.'

LAWRIE MCMENEMY, England assistant manager, soon after the Gulf War, *1992*.

I deplore the practice of sacking managers willy-nilly despite the fact that two have been sacked in the 18 months I've been here.

MIKE BATESON, Torquay chairman, *1990*.

When I said that Ossie's job wasn't on the line I meant every word. But we ran some projections through the computer which confirmed that this club would not exist if we are relegated.

> SIR JOHN HALL, Newcastle chairman, explaining why he had dismissed Ossie Ardiles as manager three days after saying his job was safe, *1992*.

I've just been upstairs to give my chairman [Fred Reacher] a vote of confidence.

> BRIAN CLOUGH, Nottingham Forest manager, *1992*.

In Halifax we are getting rid of the assumption that football clubs are the preserve of white middle-class men in camel coats, sipping champagne and using the game as an extension of their own egos and virility.

> DAVE HELLIWELL, Leader of Calderdale Council, the owners of Halifax Town, *1990*.

Those of us who involve ourselves at this level are crazy.

> COLIN HANCOCK, dentist and Aldershot chairman, *1990*.

He's a bit upset but he'll get used to it.

> HANCOCK, on 19-year-old Spencer Trethewy's first match after 'saving' debt-ridden Aldershot – a 4–0 defeat at Rochdale, *1990*.

I won't be afraid to confront any player not giving 100 per cent or pulling his weight because he might be wanting a transfer to Liverpool or somewhere. People who cross me will see me going to war.

> SPENCER TRETHEWY, property developer and 'saviour' of Aldershot, *1990*.

After the first board meeting it was obvious that he doesn't know anything about running a football club, but he got the publicity he wanted.

> COLIN HANCOCK, as Trethewy failed to produce the money he had promised, *1990*.

I entered as just A.N. Other, a member of the board, simply to do a job, i.e. finance director. No loyalty or love, simply a cold, clean, clinical job. But I ended up falling in love like the rest of you – which became the most expensive love life man can imagine.

> REG BREALEY, Sheffield United chairman, message to supporters, *1990*.

If Blues lose I cannot eat – and this is me, the businessman, who is supposed to be sensible and take things in his stride.

> SAMESH KUMAR, Birmingham chairman and fashion entrepreneur, *1990*.

What can I say? I'd better be careful – I might use a few adjectives here.

TERRY WOOD, Scarborough chairman, asked how he felt at moment club clinched promotion to Football League, *1987*.

Salman Rushdie just phoned to tell me that I'm bad news and he doesn't want anything more to do with me.

WALLACE MERCER, Hearts chairman, after receiving a bullet in the post during his takeover bid for Hibs, 1990.

I always answer letters from supporters. It's the death threats I object to.

REG BURR, Millwall chairman, *1990*.

Bill Bell: Chairman and business entrepreneur, dedicated to making Port Vale the No. 1 team in the Potteries, Bill also wants to find the lost city of Atlantis, be the first man to walk the Channel, and skateboard up Mount Everest.

THE OATCAKE, Stoke fanzine, 'derby day edition', *1989*.

The owner of the club had never been in football before – he was a solicitor. It was really a personality clash. He had no personality.

MALCOLM ALLISON, former manager, looking back on his sacking by Fisher Athletic, *1992*.

You see managers making demands. You hear players making demands. It's about time directors started making demands.

SIR JOHN HALL, Newcastle chairman, *1991*.

Even the most brilliant football manager could not deal with Manchester United as long as the club is run from the chairman's office in the way that it is.

MICHAEL CRICK and DAVID SMITH, authors, *Betrayal of a Legend*, *1989*.

Building a team now is very, very difficult. Managers are getting squeezed from all directions. The structure of players' contracts is a problem, and on top of that there is the advent of the chief executive/managing director/interfering chairman.

GRAHAM TAYLOR, England manager, *1991*.

At a time when he complains of too many League games I see he is planning more and more friendly matches at international level. When Graham Taylor pays the players' wages he can call the tune.

KEN BATES, Chelsea chairman, programme column, *1992*.

When you make Ken Bates's programme notes, it is a sign that you have really arrived.

GRAHAM TAYLOR, *1992*.

The chairman [Leslie Silver] has been absolutely magnificent . . . . He took me on 15 months ago and all along I have had nothing other than 10 per cent support.

EVERTON programme, misquoting Leeds manager Howard Wilkinson, *1990*.

I'll be expecting a 10 per cent discount after that.

SIR JACK HAYWARD, prospective buyer of Wolves, after 3–1 defeat by Port Vale, *1990*.

We've only signed him to help the board out of their financial problems.

DAVE BASSETT, Sheffield United manager, on buying commodity broker Paul Rodgers from Sutton United, *1991*.

In my three years as a director, the club won six trophies. I had a five-year plan; we achieved all but the title in 18 months.

MICHAEL KNIGHTON, Carlisle chairman, looking back on his 'successes' as a Manchester United director, *1992*.

There's only one United – Carlisle United.

KNIGHTON taking over as chairman of the Third Division club, *1992*.

'Candle in the wind' remains one of my favourite songs. But we had this agreement, Elton [John] and I, that I would tell him nothing about music if he told me nothing about football. And it worked well.

GRAHAM TAYLOR, England manager, on his former Watford chairman, *1991*.

The real power lies with the club chairmen who are, on the whole, a deeply unimpressive bunch of mediocrities. With inflammatory threats of legal action and an obdurate refusal to rise above their own self-interest they bring to industrial relations all the enlightened attitudes of nineteenth-century mill-owners.

PATRICK COLLINS, columnist, *Mail on Sunday*, *1992*.

When Tommy [Docherty] does his rounds of after-dinner speaking he uses me at every opportunity. Greavsie calls me 'Deadly', and kids in the street shout: 'Oi, Deadly!' As long as Aston Villa's name is attached to it, I don't mind. If you operate at a high profile, you have to accept criticism.

DOUG ELLIS, Aston Villa chairman, *1991*.

He's the Fidel Castro of football, an enlightened despot rather than a dictator.

STEVE COPPELL, Crystal Palace manager, on his chairman Ron Noades, *1992*.

Castro has done all right for Cuba. He [Noades] is single-minded. If you confuse dictatorship with single-mindedness, he's guilty of that charge.

COPPELL, during his chairman's dispute with two directors, *1992*.

I'd rather die and have vultures eat my inside than merge with Crystal Palace.

> SAM HAMMAM, Wimbledon chairman, on reports of possible merger between the two Selhurst Park-based clubs, *1992*.

I'm absolutely gutted. The man [chairman Stan Flashman] is a complete and utter shit, a disgrace to the game.

> BARRY FRY, after his seventh and last sacking as Barnet manager, *1992*. Fry was later reinstated.

It's quite difficult dealing with Mr Flashman, because if you speak your mind he tends to sack you. I've been sacked three times now.

> EDWIN STEIN, assistant manager of Barnet, *1992*.

If you didn't know him you'd think he was an absolute ignorant pig. He is in many ways, but he does care about the club.

> BARRY FRY on Flashman, *1992*.

I could find a better bloody chairman than [Peter] Swales. I think he's past it. He's over the bloody hill. Hey, I didn't think he was good enough to get the job in the first place.

> BRIAN CLOUGH, Nottingham Forest manager, *1992*. Swales, the Manchester City and FA International Committee chairman, had said it was too late for Clough to be England manager.

When I was at places like West Brom and Arsenal, they knew they couldn't win all the time, and they understood about patience and a consistent policy. Somehow chairmen seemed to be less ambitious for themselves. They didn't go in for self-promotion the way so many do today. Now their definition of success is making money, as quickly as possible. You talk to them about development, about how three-quarters of Arsenal's team have come up through the youth system, and they say, 'Great, let's have a youth policy, and in the meantime could you win us the FA Cup?'

> DON HOWE, after being sacked as QPR manager, *1991*.

I can't believe it. They [the board] said the allocation is 24 for me, the players and the rest of the staff. I think, as manager of this club, they could have said, 'We'll try to get you 25.'

> BRIAN CLOUGH, Nottingham Forest manager, on his FA Cup Final ticket allocation, *1991*.

The management committee are bungling, bumbling idiots.

> ROBERT MAXWELL as the Football League management committee insisted he had to sell Derby before buying Spurs, *1990*.

I've got lots of other ideas, but at the League's rate of progress one every five years is probably the most they can digest.

> KEN BATES, Chelsea chairman, acclaiming the Zenith Data Systems Cup as a success, *1990*.

Opposing fans would come to White Hart Lane and chant 'Where's your money gone?' I used to sit on the bench hoping they'd tell me.

> TERRY VENABLES, Tottenham managing director, looking back at the club's financial problems, *1992*.

Every time we open a door, it seems another IOU falls out.

> MEMBER of the Venables consortium during negotiations over the sale of the club, *1991*.

I am not a football fanatic, but I have a certain affection for Spurs.

> **ALAN SUGAR, computer mogul, on his takeover of Tottenham with Venables, pictured two years before their bitter fall-out, *1991*.**

I'll look after the £11 million at the bank while Terry Venables will look after the 11 players on the pitch.

> SUGAR, as above

I feel like the guy who shot Bambi. I am not an egotistical loony.

> SUGAR as fans protested against him when he tried to sack Venables, *1993*.

If they ran the law of the land, it would be a mugger's paradise.

> MIKE BATESON, Torquay chairman, on the FA after they decided not to punish Brentford's Gary Blissett for breaking John Uzzell's cheek with his elbow, *1992*.

It's a con job. Who pays for the policing of the Notting Hill Carnival or demonstrations at Trafalgar Square? The Government, not the organisers. Why should football be different?

> KEN BATES, Chelsea chairman, on a dramatic rise in policing charges for football, *1991*.

I don't know the president of Juventus. Isn't he a car salesman?

> BRIAN CLOUGH, Nottingham Forest manager, reacting to Fiat-backed Juventus's attempts to buy Des Walker, *1990*.

My advice to him [Venables] is 'leave football and join the lifeguards if you think you are so good at rescues'.

> GIANMARCO CALLERI, Lazio president, on Venables' efforts to stop Gascoigne's transfer by refinancing stricken Spurs, *1991*.

The club committee would be happy to be relegated to the Midland Combination as long as they had free drinks and free crisps. God help the next manager going there.

> PHIL SHARPE, Sutton Coldfield Town manager, resigning from the Beazer Homes League club, *1992*.

A few of us want to discuss super leagues but all the rest can talk about is the price of meat pies.

> DAVID MURRAY, Rangers' owner, on his fellow Scottish League chairmen, *1992*.

A LEAGUE OF THEIR OWN

When the tablets finally come down from the mountain I hope they don't simply contain a mirage of a land of milk and honey where everyone is better off.

GORDON TAYLOR, chief executive of the Professional Footballers' Association, awaiting publication of the FA's *Blueprint for the Future of Football*, in which plans for a breakaway Premier League were unveiled, *1991*.

People can have blueprints until they're blue in the face.

GORDON TAYLOR, *1991*.

It's not just about greed.

RICK PARRY, then spokesman for the First Division clubs and later chief executive of the FA Premier League, after proposed breakaway was announced, *1991*.

People think there must be a lot of my thinking in this [the Premier League]. There is none, and I'm not totally convinced this is for the betterment of the England team. I think a lot of this is based on greed.

GRAHAM TAYLOR, England manager and ex-Grimsby and Scunthorpe player, *1991*.

I do not find it acceptable that the First Division should be hijacked. It's upsetting and divisive and brings all the aggro back to the fore again.

BILL FOX, Blackburn chairman and president of the Football League, on the FA's initial plan for an 18-club Premier League, *1991*.

I guess we kicked a sleeping dog and it's up and barking.

TREVOR PHILLIPS, Football League commercial director, on FA proposals to set up a Premier League in response to League proposals to amalgamate the two bodies, *1991*.

How, for instance, could the FA exercise just one of its activities, discipline, over the Football League if it were not in itself a separate entity? We would be disciplining ourselves.

GRAHAM KELLY, FA chief executive, ruling out a merger between the League and FA, *1991*.

A merger of the FA and Football League would be like putting two dinosaurs together and getting a dodo.

GORDON TAYLOR, PFA chief executive, *1991*.

What's to do? I'll tell you what's to do. The big clubs want all the money, that's what's to do.

BILL FOX, Blackburn chairman and Football League president, opposing the split, *1991*.

The Big Five are holding a gun at everyone's head and saying 'Either join us or we'll blow you away.' You have to be swept along with that, but all I can see this doing is making the rich clubs richer. Eventually that will destroy the grass roots of the game.

STEVE COPPELL, Crystal Palace manager, *1991*.

We are not going to be raped. Without us they are sterile.

> MARTIN LANGE, Brentford chairman and spokesman for Third and Fourth Division clubs, *1991*.

It will not be a matter of isolating the top teams from the lower teams completely. When Coventry, or anyone else for that matter, is casting around for talent, it will still be looking around the Oldhams and Halifaxes of this world.

> JOHN POYNTON, Coventry chairman, defending the breakaway, *1991*. Oldham were also founder members the following year.

The evolution and management of the game have been in neutral for the past 100 years, but today's decision should send it into overdrive, rewarding all clubs, large and small.

> DAVID DEIN, Arsenal vice-chairman and arch-advocate of the Premier League, after the FA's High Court victory over the Football League, *1991*.

People who talk of the good of the game are often thinking of the good of themselves.

> GRAHAM TAYLOR, England manager, after the High Court decision, *1991*.

It's the usual cock-up. What's going to happen to the 72 clubs left behind? We've heard stories about clubs going to the wall, but this is reality.

> BILL FOX, Blackburn chairman and Football League president, *1991*.

The worst thing to happen to football for a long time. It puts a big question mark over the future of football in years to come. If you want a system where the big three win the title year after year then carry on.

> STEVE COPPELL, Crystal Palace manager, *1991*.

If this proposed Super League leaves shore without the players on board it will sink. People don't turn up to watch chairmen.

> GORDON TAYLOR, PFA chief executive, warning of strike action if the players were not consulted, *1991*.

A players' strike is out of the question. It's just a ritual dance of the sort you expect from unions.

> SIR JOHN QUINTON, Barclays Bank and Premier League chairman, *1991*.

If he thinks he can treat footballers like his bank tellers, then he's in for a shock.

> GORDON TAYLOR, responding to Sir John.

I see Gordon Taylor is asking his players to strike. I've been asking mine to strike since New Year's Day.

> RON ATKINSON, Aston Villa manager, after his team scored only once in 15 hours' play, *1992*.

I'm off back to my pigsty. You meet a better class of person there.

> KEN BATES, Chelsea chairman, as a Premier League meeting broke up acrimoniously over sponsorship and alleged secret deals, *1992*.

The whole concept of one club one vote is proving unworkable. We have hit a brick wall with something of a thud.

> RICK PARRY, Premier League chief executive, as the clubs split into two warring factions over sponsorship and TV, *1992*.

We were there in force, but the chairman of the Premier League wasn't there and wasn't contactable, and another representative left at lunchtime.

> GORDON TAYLOR, PFA chief executive, on the difficulties of negotiating with the Premier League, *1992*.

We have been asked to support a concept that was supposed to be about quality, but looks to me to be about money.

> GORDON TAYLOR, *1992*.

The Premier League planned for next season will be a waste of time as long as there are 22 teams competing in it. I can't see why they are bothering with the change. It seems to me there are some people in positions of power who are more set on massaging personal egos than concerning themselves with what would be good for the game.

> GARY LINEKER, Spurs and England forward, *1991*.

You'll find the big clubs with financial clout like Derby will get back-up, the small clubs will disappear and then it's a rich elite subdivided into two groups. Whatever you think of the morality of the Premier League, the reality is that you've got to be in it. There's a big black hole beneath it.

> LENNIE LAWRENCE, Middlesbrough manager, *1992*.

For Notts [County] to endorse the Premier League is like a cow advocating meat-eating.

> SATURDAY NIGHT & SUNDAY MORNING, Nottingham-based fanzine, *1991*.

A 22-headed monster.

> GORDON TAYLOR, PFA chief executive, *1992*.

CHAPTER 12

Grounds for Devotion and Despair

Abbey Stadium (Cambridge United)

Arsenal had Highbury and big stars and huge crowds and the whole weight of history on their backs; Cambridge had a tiny, ramshackle little ground, the Abbey Stadium (their equivalent of the Clock End was the Allotments End, and occasionally, naughty visiting fans would nip round the back of it and hurl pensioners' cabbages over the wall), less than 4000 watching at most games, and no history at all.

NICK HORNBY, author, *Fever Pitch: A Fan's Life, 1992.*

Anfield (Liverpool)

With every stride that takes you nearer Liverpool FC's home ground, every second that brings you nearer kick-off time, the noise from the Kop and the assault on the eye of red everywhere – on scarves, hats, banners, badges, faces – makes it ever more certain that you know precisely where you are and why. This is not Hartlepool, or Hull, and it is certainly not Heaven. That 'This is Anfield' sign is intended to have precisely the same effect upon strangers as the words 'Welcome to Death Row' would have to a condemned criminal. It tells you that now there's no turning back.

BRIAN JAMES, author, *Journey to Wembley, 1977.*

Baseball Ground (Derby County)

The tight, terraced streets which hemmed in the ground for decades may have disappeared, but inside there is still that almost claustrophobic atmosphere, and there is nowhere quite like it with a full house for a big match.

ANTON RIPPON and ANDREW WARD, co-authors, *The Derby County Story, 1983.*

Bescot Stadium (Walsall)

Since Walsall's new ground is to be built on the site of an old sewage works, may I suggest the name W.C. Fields?

> LETTER to *Sports Argus*, Birmingham, who had sought suggestions for a name for the stadium, *1989.*

I have seen the future and it is a warehouse without a roof. Walsall's Christmas-morning new home had the wrapping snatched off it on Saturday and what did we find but Legoland.

> ANDY COLQUHOUN, football correspondent, *Birmingham Post, 1990.*

Broomfield Park (Airdrieonians)

A cauldron of apathy.

> DAVID LIVINGSTONE, journalist, *The Independent, 1992.*

Craven Cottage (Fulham)

Here is Craven Cottage in the rain with the wind drifting across the banks of the Thames on the popular side, blowing dinghies downstream so that their masts wobble above the advertising boards and the half-time scoreboard which nobody can understand . . . [It] is a pretty ground which was once the home of Bulwer Lytton, and where he wrote *The Last Days of Pompeii*, a point often used by tired journalists to fill up space.

> JOHN MOYNIHAN, author, *The Soccer Syndrome, 1966.*

Dalymount Park, Dublin

It's a bit like a Third Division ground, innit? Gets a coat of paint every two years.

> DAVID KELLY, Republic of Ireland striker, after scoring his fourth goal in two games for Ireland at Dalymount, *1990.*

The Den (Millwall)

Teams hate coming to The Den. I remember going there with York City for my first visit. It took us half an hour to find the place. Eventually we went up this dingy back street. I remember thinking, 'Where is this?' Then you go and have a look at the pitch, which is bumpy, terrible. The away team dressing room is a dungeon, no light, no window. The bathrooms are horrible. Then you get out there to face them – the Lions. And they come storming at you and most sides jack it in . . . When you have been there a little time, though, you grow to love it. It's one of our biggest assets.

> EAMON DUNPHY, Millwall and Republic of Ireland midfielder, in *Only a Game?, 1976.*

Elland Road (Leeds United)

Probably the most intimidating ground in Europe.

ALEX FERGUSON, Manchester United manager, after League Cup semi-final at Leeds, *1991*.

Foxboro Stadium, Boston

If it can survive Guns 'n' Roses, it can survive a soccer match.

GUIDO TOGNONI, FIFA press officer, on the suitability of Foxboro as a World Cup venue, *1992*.

Hampden Park, Glasgow

The great grandfather of sound, at Hampden Park, can still be as fearsome as ever, making visiting players pale and sick with the feeling that each one of 120,000 throats is a spear aimed for his stomach.

JOHN MOYNIHAN, author, *Soccer Syndrome, 1966*.

The fourth worst international stadium in the world, just behind those of Latvia, the Solomon Islands and Gibraltar.

THE FINAL HURDLE, Dundee United fanzine, *1991*.

The only ground which looks the same in black and white as it does in colour.

DAVID LACEY, **football correspondent,** *The Guardian, 1987*.

Hampden continues to creak in the wind.

> GLASGOW HERALD, at time of publication of Taylor Report, *1990*.

Highbury (Arsenal)

A symbol of a bygone age and an example of fine architecture.

> SIMON INGLIS, author, *The Football Grounds of Great Britain*, on the pre-modernised Arsenal Stadium, *1987*.

Hillsborough (Sheffield Wednesday)

This is still the place to buy boiled sweets at the corner shop, wear a rosette with pride but then go and watch in comfort. Indeed, a visit to Hillsborough on a crisp, autumn afternoon remains one of the quintessential joys of English sport.

> SIMON INGLIS, author, *The Football Grounds of Great Britain, 1987.*

An alp of humanity.

> PATRICK BARCLAY, journalist, *The Independent,* on the old terraced Kop, *1987.*

The only safe stadium in my view is an empty one.

> DR STEFAN POPPER, South Yorkshire coroner, at the Hillsborough inquest, *1991.*

Ibrox Stadium (Rangers)

At Ibrox the next day there were 42,000, three stands of blue against one of green – and the outpost of green was awash with the Irish tricolour. An awesome noise of defiance rose up from among them – and when the players came out the sound was volcanic, totally deafening. Who says all-seaters damp down the passion? Not here – you felt the glory and the animal both stirring in your gut.

> PETE DAVIES, author, in *All Played Out: The Full Story of Italia '90, 1990.*

Giuseppe Meazza Stadium (Milan)

It's an unbelievable stadium. At first there were two tiers, but for the Mondiale, they bolted another tier on top, then put a roof on top of that. It's not pretty, it's a great fierce box of a place – four vast steep walls of seats sweep down towards you, it's intimidating – and it's electric . . . . It's by Spielberg out of Orwell. It seats 80,000 and it's the closest encounter you'll get to the future of football.

> PETE DAVIES, author, *All Played Out: The Full Story of Italia '90, 1990.*

Behold the new Giuseppe Meazza Stadium in San Siro, Milan; a gargantuan concrete, steel and glass temple to the great god of 'calcio'.

> SIMON INGLIS, author, *The Football Grounds of Europe, 1990.*

Blimey, the ground looks a bit different to Watford. Where's the dog track?

> LUTHER BLISSETT, England striker, after joining AC Milan from Watford, *1983*.

It is a potato patch.

> JÜRGEN KLINSMANN, Inter Milan forward, on the problems with the San Siro pitch after the World Cup, *1991*.

Nou Camp Stadium (Barcelona)

Full to the brim, the Nou Camp presents us with a wall of humanity. When a drum sounds from one of the small terraced areas behind each goal, the plunging bowl itself becomes a drum, reverberating with sound.

> SIMON INGLIS, author, *The Football Grounds of Europe, 1990*.

Oakwell (Barnsley)

How can I think about playing Barnsley at Oakwell now that I've seen the Olympic Stadium?

> KEVIN MORAN, Blackburn and Republic of Ireland defender, returning to reality after the World Cup quarter-final v Italy in Rome, *1990*.

Old Trafford (Manchester United)

It's the only stadium in the world I've ever been in that's absolutely buzzing with atmosphere when it's empty and there isn't a soul inside. It's almost like a cathedral.

> TOMMY DOCHERTY, former United manager, in *Call the Doc, 1982*.

The theatre of dreams.

> ALEX FERGUSON, United manager, *1986*.

For Manchester United's Red Army, the Stretford End was their barracks. Like the old Hill at Sydney, or Liverpool's Kop, it contained doctors of working-class philosophy.

> GRAHAM FISHER, journalist, *Today*, on the demolition of United's famous 'end', *1992*.

A sound trap of red and white aggression.

> SIMON INGLIS, author, *The Football Grounds of Great Britain, 1987*.

Parkhead (Celtic)

Whereas Ibrox is a stately home, Parkhead is a down-to-earth people's palace.

> SIMON INGLIS, author, *The Football Grounds of Great Britain, 1987*.

Selhurst Park (Crystal Palace/Wimbledon)

Perhaps if it had been at the Stretford End or the Kop it would have been given – but not at the Sainsbury's End.

STEVE COPPELL, Crystal Palace manager, after being refused a late penalty, *1989*.

The place is like a morgue. Most of those that did come are moaning bastards. There's no home advantage for us.

JOE KINNEAR, Wimbledon manager, after only 1987 turned up for Coca-Cola Cup match v Bolton, *1992*.

St Andrews (Birmingham City)

We have worked very hard to win an international reputation for Birmingham, and yet the club with our name is a place of flaking paint, rust and filth.

BRYAN BIRD, city councillor and Birmingham fan, *1989*.

Stadium of Light (Benfica)

The oval pitch area is, unusually, entirely grassed, with not even a sliver of a perimeter track. It is like looking down into the crater of a volcano, half-filled by a deep, still, green pool. Gradually, one begins to see why the stadium is so aptly named. There is hardly a shadow in the entire arena.

SIMON INGLIS, author, *The Football Grounds of Europe, 1990*.

Stamford Bridge (Chelsea)

Stamford Bridge, that great, ungainly bowl with the dripping wet greyhound track round the edges of the pitch, the great slug of immovable terracing on the popular side, and the advertising posters behind the goal, and the old, rusty main stand on our right, filled with pale faces, and the new stand, incongruous on stilts lying over one corner flag; Stamford Bridge, home of Chelsea Football Club since 1905 and still standing there after Hitler's war.

JOHN MOYNIHAN, author, *The Soccer Syndrome, 1966*.

[Peter Osgood, David Webb and I] left behind us that newly completed monstrosity of a stand – I still think the fans got the worst of the deal; it got rusty long before Ossie, Webby and I.

ALAN HUDSON, former Chelsea and England player, in *Call Me a Player*, an unpublished autobiography, *1991*.

Twerton Park (Bath City/Bristol Rovers)

I call it the Azteca Stadium.

> BOBBY GOULD, Bristol Rovers manager, on the club's ground-sharing arrangement with non-League Bath, *1987*.

If we've got enough firewood there might even be some warm showers for them afterwards.

> GEOFF DUNFORD, Bristol Rovers director, on the welcome Liverpool could expect at Rovers' temporary home, *1992*.

Vale Park (Port Vale)

It's ironic that an area renowned for decorative and delicate Wedgwood and Spode could spawn a ground as bleak and unattractive as this. Nowhere have so many different shades of grey been on display at the same time.

> *FORTUNE'S ALWAYS HIDING*, West Ham fanzine, *1991*.

The Valley (Charlton Athletic)

It was just a football club leaving its ground, but to many, many people it was so much more. For the older fans it was the destruction of something that had run like a thread through their lives and for those of us who knew The Valley's past only at second hand it was the crushing of a dream. Charlton's moonlight flit was a cruel human tragedy that found no expression in the accountant's figures.

> RICK EVERITT, *Voice of the Valley* fanzine, *1988*.

Strange how a ground can catch hold of you. I came past The Valley tonight and found myself staring at it. All those memories! We had to go back didn't we?

> ROGER ALWEN, Charlton chairman, announcing return 'home', *1989*.

I will be saying a little prayer for the fans and Charlton chairman Roger Alwen. Their efforts have been rewarded.

> LENNIE LAWRENCE, Middlesbrough and former Charlton manager, on Charlton's return to The Valley, *1992*.

Villa Park (Aston Villa)

Even if Villa had lost that afternoon it would have made no difference. Villa Park had class. It had history. It had eccentric buildings in odd places. It had iron railings and a bowling green. Villa Park was a symbol of the old Birmingham in my sepia-tinted imagination.

> SIMON INGLIS, journalist, stadia specialist and Aston Villa fan, in Harry Lansdown and Alex Spillius (eds), *Saturday's Boys, 1990*.

White Hart Lane (Tottenham Hotspur)

The home of Tottenham Hotspur Football Club is at 748 High Road, London N17. You could easily miss it, if you were rushing down the High Road with your head down. It's set slightly back from the road with the main entrance down a little lane beside a pub, the White Hart. But once you've stepped back and taken it all in, it's hard to believe that anyone could miss it. The stadium lurks behind the High Road like a vast battleship with its floodlights towering over the rooftops for miles around.

> HUNTER DAVIES, author, *The Glory Game, 1972.*

A great place. Only one thing wrong with that ground. The seats face the pitch.

> LES DAWSON, comedian on BBC TV's *Fast Friends, 1991.*

Wembley Stadium

A vast white elephant, a rotting sepulchre of hopes and the grave of fortunes.

> NEWSPAPER description of Wembley at the closing of the British Empire Exhibition in 1925. (Quoted by David Lacey, *The Guardian, 1989*)

I've seen sexier stadiums, more spectacular stadiums and bigger stadiums, but I've been in no other stadium which on the days of a big match has quite the same flavour.

> BRIAN WOLFSON, chairman Wembley plc, announcing improvement plans, *1989.*

Venue of Legends.

> ADVERTISING slogan, *1990.*

My impression was that it was like a dried-up pigsty. There had been an American Football match there the previous week, and the place had clearly not been cleaned up. There was popcorn and dried-up lemonade everywhere as well as general debris.

> HUGH EDWARDS, treasurer of Aston Villa Shareholders' Association, after seeing his team in Makita Tournament, *1990.*

If Wembley was a beach, the EC would make it fly the skull and crossbones from the twin towers. If it was near Sellafield, British Nuclear Fuels would complain about the pollution.

> JONATHAN FOSTER, journalist, *The Independent*, on the national stadium's 'overflowing loos', *1991.*

It's a wonderful, wonderful place, the best in the world when you win. But when you lose it looks dirty and empty.

> OSSIE ARDILES, West Brom manager, after winning the Second Division play-off final, *1993.*

USA: The Finals Frontier

No thanks, give it to the sports desk.

> NEWS EDITOR, ABC radio network, on being offered the story that the USA had been awarded the 1994 World Cup finals, *1990*.

The World Cup. They call it soccer. I call it recess.

> PATRICK REUSSE, columnist, *Minneapolis Star-Tribune, 1990.*

North America is the last frontier for the game to conquer. Everything here in '94, from hotels, to pitches, to medical facilities will be A-plus. Having said that, not too many people in this country care that the World Cup is coming.

> RODNEY MARSH, chief executive of Tampa Bay Rowdies and former England player, *1992.*

Maybe it's just paranoia, but I can see newspapers and TV stations running pictures of the Heysel disaster or a riot somewhere and asking people, 'Is this what you want in your backyard?'

> JOHN KERR, director of Major Indoor Soccer League Players' Association, *1990.*

Public enthusiasm in the United States for the 1994 World Cup is about the same as it is for the Communist Party.

> ARCHIE MACPHERSON, columnist and broadcaster, in *Sunday Mail* column, *1992.*

I think the reason people are going to love to see the World Cup in the US is because it is a different show.

> PELE, *1992.*

America's most popular sports: 31st, Tractor pulling; 61st, Beach volleyball; 75th, Soccer; 113th, Cricket.

> LOS ANGELES TIMES list of 114 sports in order of popularity, *1991.*

Biathlon. Luge. Soccer. Three of a kind.

> THE PLAINS DEALER newspaper, Ohio, comparing the World Cup finals with the Winter Olympics for 'pointlessness and trivia enhancement', *1990.*

In Europe, as in South America, they go raving mad over the game. Pray that it doesn't happen here. The way to beat it is constant vigilance and rigid control. If soccer shows signs of getting too big, swat it down.

> PRESCOTT SULLIVAN, columnist, *San Francisco Examiner*, on advent of the North American Soccer League, 1974, quoted in Colin Jose, *NASL: A Complete Record,* 1989.

When I played in the NASL for Vancouver Whitecaps in 1977 I was told: 'The trouble with you English is that you're so hidebound by tradition. We know how to sell the game.' So they got chimpanzees and female parachutists delivering the match-ball, and the late Trevor Hockey's team had him in a tank dressed as Fidel Castro.

> GORDON TAYLOR, PFA chief executive, on American-inspired proposals to FIFA to change width of goals and make it a game of four quarters, *1990.*

Tell the Kraut to get his ass up front. We don't pay a million for a guy to hang around in defense.

> NEW YORK COSMOS executive on Franz Beckenbauer's tendency to play deep, *1970s.*

The owners never understood what went on between the two penalty areas.

> STEVE HUNT, English former Cosmos player, looking back on the NASL's demise, *1990.*

Because in this bloody country, Americans think that any guy who runs around in shorts kicking a ball instead of catching it has to be a Commie or a fairy.

> CLIVE TOYE, Cosmos British general manager, on why the club gave away so many 'promos' and 'freebies', *1970.*

When I presented my passport at Immigration they looked me up and down and said: 'No, no way', I asked what was wrong and they pointed at me, laughing. '*You?* A footballer?' To them it meant big guys in helmets and shoulder pads. I had to explain that I was a soccer player before they let me in.

> MICKEY THOMAS, Wrexham and former Wichita Wings indoor 'soccer player', *1992.*

North American sports such as baseball, American football and ice hockey have natural breaks in the action which are ideal for slotting in television commercials. Not so soccer. Thus, the moguls of the TV industry decided, with the co-operation of the referee, to orchestrate their own breaks. Only four weeks into the season it was discovered that 11 of the 21 free-kicks awarded by referee Peter Rhodes in the game between Toronto and Pittsburgh were called to allow CBS to fit in its commercials.

> COLIN JOSE, football historian, recalling inaugural season (1973) of NASL in *North American Soccer League: A Complete Record, 1989.*

With such refinements as a thirty-five-yard offside law, synthetic pitches which are not conducive to tackling, 'shoot-outs' to eliminate drawn games and bonus points, the country which gave the world Disneyland has provided a Mickey Mouse football industry.

> JACK ROLLIN, editor, on the NASL in *Rothman's Football Year Book, 1979–80*.

Soccer is a game in which everyone does a lot of running around . . . . Mostly, twenty-one guys stand around and one guy does a tap dance with the ball. It's about as exciting as *Tristan and Isolde.*

> JIM MURRAY, *Louisville Courier Journal, 1967.*

Those Stoker guys are so cocky they make me mad saying ours is a dull game. Boy, if ours is dull, theirs is even duller. Those nuts. Running around in shorts, chasing a big ball like a bunch of schoolboys.

> JOE AZCUE, Cleveland Indians baseball coach, *1967*. Cleveland Stokers were Stoke City.

Winning the world title, as the American women's team recently did, was something of a two-edged sword. On the one hand, an undoubted achievement. On the other, a marvellous propaganda ploy for American opponents of the game who could thus brand it as a game for girls.

> BRIAN GLANVILLE, sports columnist, *The People, 1992.*

The indoor game definitely provides more what the American fan wants to see. The outdoor game is better, there's more strategy and tactics. But in America they like a winner and they like action. It's like the ice hockey – I went to a game which was more like a fight and that's what the crowd love. They like the physical stuff.

> KEITH WELLER, ex-England player with Fort Lauderdale Strikers, *1983.*

Americans, whatever our flaws, have been masters of developing more complex and advanced games. Not only are our favorites – baseball, [gridiron] football and basketball – three of the most engaging and exciting games ever played on the planet, but we have literally invented more great games than we need. We will of course watch soccer in the improved form of ice hockey, which is soccer speeded up to the point where it becomes semi-interesting.

> *THE PHILADELPHIA INQUIRER, 1990.*

If we'd played them at outdoor soccer the scores would probably have been reversed.

> KENNY COOPER, Baltimore Blast coach, after 8–3 win over Sheffield Wednesday in indoor, six-a-side match, *1992.*

We're not good enough to win the World Cup. We'll probably lose to Italy on penalties in the final . . . .

> BOB GANSLER, US coach, before World Cup finals, *1990.*

A calf stands a better chance of winning a rodeo than the US has of beating Italy.

> MIKE DOWNEY, *Los Angeles Times* journalist, before the Americans' 1–0 defeat by the hosts, *1990*.

If we lived in another country we'd be asking for political asylum. But since we're American we'll stay in New York and nobody will recognise us.

> TAB RAMOS, US midfielder, after 5–1 defeat by Czechoslovakia at World Cup, *1990*.

The game went into overtime and, in the last minute, David Platt flipped in a foul shot by Paul Gascoigne.

> AMERICAN agency description of Platt's winner for England v Belgium, World Cup finals, *1990*.

Winning Ugly, Losing Ugly, Just Plain Ugly

> NEW YORK TIMES headline on World Cup Final, West Germany v Argentina, *1990*.

They're going to bring this thing to the USA in 1994 and charge money for people to watch it? Listen, if this thing were a Broadway show it would have closed after one night.

> FRANK DEPFORD, editor-columnist of *The National*, at the World Cup Final, *1990*.

A confrontation at Anfield Road between Liverpool and Tottenham fanatics is like a confrontation between the Crypts and the Bloods in a New York suburb, with sticks, chains and knives.

> SOCCER USA magazine, *1993*.

What's the first word to come into your head when I say 'British soccer fan'? It was 'subhuman' wasn't it? I rest my case.

> THE PHILADELPHIA INQUIRER, questioning the wisdom of the USA hosting the 1994 finals, *1990*.

No one on my sports desk gives a shit about soccer . . . . Someone wrote an article about John Harkes going to Sheffield Wednesday and the editor changed it to 'going to Sheffield, Wednesday'.

> DAVID WALDSTEIN, *New York Post* journalist and soccer fan, *1993*.

John Harkes will be the first American to set cleat upon Wembley's storied pitch to play a game of soccer there.

> NATIONAL SPORTS DAILY profile by Ian Thomsen, *1991*.

I thought I knew everything about English soccer, but I had never heard of a team called Wednesday or a place called Sheffield. I had to look them up pretty quickly. Then I imagined I might be able to pop back and see my folks at Christmas. I had to tell them the bad news on the phone. They'd never heard of Boxing Day.

JOHN HARKES, **Sheffield Wednesday's American international midfielder,** *1990.*

I love Christmas in New Jersey, and it would be nice to have a short break like some other countries but I can already hear the manager's reaction to my suggesting that. He'd say: 'Harksey, are you Americans all soft, or what?'

HARKES, *1990.* Wednesday's manager at the time was Ron Atkinson.

I shouted to one lad to take on the full-back just for a change, and he stopped to say he'd always been taught to pass in those situations. I shouted back, 'but you're the bloody left winger!'

RODNEY MARSH, Tampa Bay Rowdies, on the effects of college-football coaching on American players, *1991.*

Scott LeTellier, chief operating officer of the 1994 finals, said: 'We have evidence that it will not be a problem to grow grass indoors. Millions of Americans have been doing it for years, but they don't usually play football on it.'

> FOOTIE magazine's reporting on the prospect of matches at Michigan's covered Pontiac Silverdome during the 1994 finals, *1990*.

To say that American soccer is the football of the future is ludicrous. You've got to see football in the black townships of South Africa or Rio before you can talk about the football of the future.

> JACK TAYLOR, English World Cup referee, *1978*.

If the US becomes enthralled by soccer it will be when every back street and stretch of urban waste ground has its teams of kids playing their makeshift matches, the players claiming the temporary identity of the world's stars in the sport. Environments like that produce those stars. Football is an inner compulsion. It cannot be settled on a people like instant coffee.

> ARTHUR HOPCRAFT, author, *The Football Man, 1968*.

Will the World Cup transform America into a nation of soccer lovers? For the life of me, I can't imagine how. One sportswriter remarked that it's difficult to imagine giddy Americans running into the streets screaming 'We tied Czechoslovakia!' It is equally difficult to visualise the schoolyards of America filled with youngsters pretending to be Jürgen Klinsmann instead of Joe Montana or Larry Bird.

> DAVE WANGERIN, American soccer writer, in *When Saturday Comes* magazine, *1990*.

I wouldn't go to America to play football, but to get away from it.

> JÜRGEN KLINSMANN, German international striker, on thoughts of retirement, *1991*.

Being event snobs, the Americans will doubtless pour into the eight stadiums as they did in the Olympic soccer tournament. Then soccer in America will go to sleep again, the preserve of the colleges, white suburban youth and the ladies.

> BRIAN GLANVILLE, columnist, *The People*, looking ahead to the World Cup finals, *1992*.

The pitches will be great, the organisation will be spot on. Michael Jackson will do his thing, and it will be brilliant. It's just that they [Americans] haven't got a clue about football.

> RODNEY MARSH, former England striker and Tampa Bay Rowdies chief executive, *1993*.

Perhaps the World Cup will be merely a one-shot deal, a chance for Europeans and Japanese to take advantage of the exchange rate and stay in our good hotels and drive our good interstates and eat fast food and try to get from Seattle to Miami when their nation advances. But we will have soccer. For five weeks we will have soccer.

> GEORGE VECSEY, columnist, *New York Times*, at World Cup draw, *1991*.

184

CHAPTER 14

Famous Last Words

For older players like Tommy Hutchison and myself this could be our final FA Cup fling. We mean to go out with a bang.

ALAN CURTIS, Swansea striker, before tie v Liverpool, *1989*. Swansea lost 8–0.

We are going to slay the dragon in his lair.

JOHN BECK, Cambridge manager, before his side's FA Cup tie at Highbury, *1991*. Arsenal won 2–1.

Touch wood, I've never scored an own goal in ten years as a professional.

DAVID MILLER, Stockport player, before scoring Derby's last-minute winner, FA Cup, *1993*.

It's now a matter of building up and trying not to become impatient. But we all know that we are, hopefully, just a month away from playing in the Final of the European Championship.

GRAHAM TAYLOR, England manager, *1992*. England did not get past the first round.

Let me get this straight – if Ron [Saunders] goes, so do I.

PETER SWALES, Manchester City chairman, *1973*. Saunders left the following year but nine managers later, Swales is still chairman.

There's not one player in your team who wants to play anywhere else – and I certainly don't want to manage anywhere else.

HOWARD KENDALL, Manchester City manager, to the clubs' fans, October *1990*. By November he was back with Everton.

I'm a Nantes player and I intend to stay so for another year when I become a free agent.

MAURICE JOHNSTON, Scotland striker, ridiculing reports of a move to Rangers, *1989*.

Certainly I won't go to Rangers. They don't sign Catholics and anyway I don't want to go to Ibrox.

JOHNSTON, a fortnight before joining Rangers, *1989*.

It's a complete fabrication. You can run that story for ten years and it still wouldn't be true.

BILL MCMURDO, Johnston's agent, on reports that Rangers wanted to sign his client – only days before they did, *1989*.

There's as much chance of [Frank] McAvennie leaving as there is of us losing 5–1 tomorrow.

BILLY MCNEILL, Celtic manager, *1988*. Celtic lost 5–1 to Rangers the following day and McAvennie eventually left.

I have two years of my contract left, and I am happy to stay at Villa.

DAVID PLATT, Aston Villa midfielder, scorning suggestions that he would leave Villa for Italy, March *1991*. He began the following season with Bari.

Why won't people believe us when we say no? We're fed up hearing the same question – everyone seems to know more than us. Where are they getting their info from?

ARCHIE KNOX, Rangers assistant manager, on speculation that the club were to re-sign Trevor Steven from Marseille, *1992*. Steven signed the following morning.

Tonight Arsenal will confirm their return to European club competition by beating Benfica – and then going on to win the League Championship and European Cup double.

KEVIN KEEGAN, former England captain, working as TV analyst, *1991*. Arsenal went out to Benfica and finished fourth in the League.

I've mended my ways. I'm no use to Celtic if I get booked every week.

PAUL ELLIOTT, Celtic defender, who was promptly cautioned in his next four matches, *1990*.

I must be barmy to think of leaving this club – I've got the best job in football. In the final analysis, I couldn't turn my back on people who have been so good to me.

RON ATKINSON, Sheffield Wednesday manager, after turning down Aston Villa, *1991*. A week later he was Villa manager.

My reasons for staying are all about what is going on at Bristol City – there is vast potential here.

JOE JORDAN, Bristol City manager, on turning down an offer from Aston Villa, *1990*. Two months later he joined Hearts.

How Davie Dodds went through the game without being spoken to, booked or sent off, is beyond me. He uses his hands so often he's more suited to volleyball. Every time Richard Gough or Terry Butcher went for a high ball they were heading his elbows.

GRAEME SOUNESS, Rangers manager, on the Aberdeen striker after a bitter match at Pittodrie, *1988*. Within a year Souness had signed Dodds for Rangers.

Bobby, of course, was twice a contender for the Chelsea managership, a job he always wanted, but on the principle that you can't have friends in partnership, there's no chance that he'll ever become manager of Chelsea.

> KEN BATES, Chelsea chairman, in *Chelsea: My Year*, when Campbell was in charge at Portsmouth, *1984*. Campbell became Chelsea manager in 1988.

I'm not here for just one season. It'd be a bloody expensive season ticket if I was.

> SPENCER TRETHEWY, 19, on his £100,000 cash injection to save Aldershot, *1990*. By the end of the season he had gone.

If anybody ever hears that Kevin Keegan is coming back to football full-time, they can laugh as much as I will. It will never happen. That is certain.

> **KEVIN KEEGAN, former England captain, leaving England to live in Marbella, *1985*.**

Let's kill off the rumours that Ossie Ardiles's job is on the line. If he leaves it will be of his own volition.

> SIR JOHN HALL, Newcastle United chairman, three days before dismissing Ardiles and installing Keegan, *1992*.

I've no intention of ever leaving this place [Ibrox]. I see my short-term and my long-term future here. I'm very fortunate to work with some great people and we are building something that will last a very long time.

> GRAEME SOUNESS, Rangers manager, two months before joining Liverpool, *1991*.

Good afternoon everyone, and yes, I am still here.

> BRIAN TALBOT, West Brom manager, in his programme notes, December *1990*. He was dismissed in the New Year.

At least you know you're alive and not half-dead from all the emotion. Now it's all come good it's a lovely feeling. See you all next season.

> JIM RYAN, Luton manager, after his team's escape from relegation, *1991*. The next day he was sacked.

I'm about as likely to buy Posh as BCCI are to fund me.

> CHRIS TURNER, Peterborough manager, shortly before he bought the club, *1992*.

It will not happen again. That defeat by Sutton United last year was our inoculation against it occurring again.

> JOHN SILLETT, Coventry manager, before his team's FA Cup exit at Fourth Division Northampton, *1990*.

I expected a negative reaction from the opposition supporters and can handle that. But the Newcastle fans were great and I want to make this club my home for some time.

> JUSTIN FASHANU, making a comeback after revealing his homosexuality, *1991*. He was released by Newcastle 24 hours later.

I expect to win. Let me do the worrying, that's what I'm paid for. You get your feet up in front of the telly, get a few beers in and have a good time.

> GRAHAM TAYLOR, England manager, before drab goalless draw v Denmark, *1992*.

Thank goodness that's over. I'm going to go out and celebrate tonight. I never want to go through that again.

> STEVE COPPELL, Crystal Palace manager, after his team's victory over Ipswich appeared to have made their Premier League place safe, *1993*. One week and three Oldham wins later, Palace were relegated and Coppell resigned.

Stockport County have made steady gains this season and there is growing optimism that Asa Hartford will guide them out of the bottom division for the first time in 21 years come 1990.

THE TIMES, 22 March *1989.*

Stockport County yesterday dismissed player-manager Asa Hartford . . . .

THE TIMES, 23 March *1989.*

No way would Ossie contemplate going into the turmoil of Spurs, with fans boycotting and players wanting out. Even if Tottenham was a happy ship I don't think he'd want to go – it's not the environment he seeks. . . . I spoke to him on Tuesday and if he'd had any doubts at all he'd have answered my questions in a negative way. But he was entirely positive and is really looking forward to next season at Albion.

TONY HALE, West Brom vice-chairman, as speculation mounted that Ossie Ardiles was to become Tottenham manager, *1993.* Within days he was in charge at White Hart Lane.

Index